Productions in Print
An imprint of Smith and Kraus Publishers, Inc.
Published by Smith and Kraus, Inc.
177 Lyme Road, Hanover, NH 03755
www.SmithandKraus.com

Copyright 2010 Amy Herzog
Contact: Val Day, WME Entertainment, LLC
1325 Avenue of the Americas
New York, NY 10019

Manufactured in the United States of America, 2010.

Artistic Direction: Bradford Louryk
Cover Layout: Emily Kent

ISBN-13: 978-1-936232-42-0
ISBN-10: 1-936232-42-1

10 9 8 7 6 5 4 3 2

PLAYWRIGHTS HORIZONS

40 ANNIVERSARY

Tim Sanford
Artistic Director

Leslie Marcus
Managing Director

Carol Fishman
General Manager

presents

AFTER THE REVOLUTION

A new play by

AMY HERZOG

Featuring

**Mark Blum   Peter Friedman   Meredith Holzman
David Margulies   Katharine Powell
Lois Smith   Elliot Villar   Mare Winningham**

Scenic Design	Costume Design	Lighting Design	Original Music & Sound Design
Clint Ramos	**Kaye Voyce**	**Ben Stanton**	**Fitz Patton**

Casting	Director of Development	Director of New Play Development
Alaine Alldaffer, CSA	**Jill Garland**	**Adam Greenfield**
MelCap Casting		

Production Manager	Press Representative	Production Stage Manager
Christopher Boll	**The Publicity Office**	**Hannah Cohen**

Directed by

CAROLYN CANTOR

The World Premiere of *After The Revolution* was commissioned, developed and produced by the Williamstown Theatre Festival, Nicholas Martin, Artistic Director.

Special thanks to the Harold and Mimi Steinberg Charitable Trust for supporting new plays at Playwrights Horizons.

Special thanks to Time Warner Inc. for its leadership support of The American Voice: New Play and Musical Theater Development at Playwrights Horizons.

Introduction:

The introduction to James Loewen's landmark study of high school history textbooks, *Lies My Teacher Told Me*, begins with a slew of dispiriting statistics about the indifference and ignorance of graduating seniors regarding history. Loewen proceeds to take apart the myths and inaccuracies promulgated in most history classes and suggests that a more nuanced analysis of history's causes and effects would play much differently to its captive audience. I was therefore most inspired and reassured to read a new play by an exciting young writer, *After the Revolution* by Amy Herzog, that fervently engages the underlying complexity and ambiguity of history.

The historical problem at the play's center resides in the larger;than-life stature of the family patriarch, Joe Joseph, a prominent Marxist activist blacklisted by McCarthy's HUAC hearings. The primary standard-bearer and eventual questioner of that history is the brilliant recent law school graduate, Emma, who carries forth her grandfather's activist heritage by founding a legal defense fund in his name to fight for the exoneration of former Black Panther/convicted cop-killer Mumia Abu-Jamal, on Death Row since 1981.When Emma learns from her father and uncle that some disturbing information about Joe is about to surface, everything changes: her view of history, her relationship with her father, and her goals for the future.

Revolutionaries and their kin—progressives and activists—espouse change. But can we? We elected a president who campaigned on a promise of change. But one of Playwrights Horizons' most popular plays from last season, Bruce Norris's *Clybourne Park,* essentially mocked the notion of change. Aren't the dialectics of change two steps forward, one step back one year, then one step forward, two steps back the next? And is there any social ecosystem that dramatizes this dynamic more than the family? Isn't it a truism that we vow to break free of our families, to create new families that repudiate ingrained family habits only to reestablish the same habits in different forms in our own? So it is very fitting that *After the Revolution* is also very much a family play. The nexus of history that Emma must struggle to solve or escape resides in her grandfather. At the very same time that her father and her grandfather's widow espouse radical change, they also urge Emma to hold onto Joe's legacy, to honor it, to keep the status quo. There's a human cost to progress, but isn't the cost of not changing even steeper?

It is rare to find a scope of vision so broad and deep in any writer, much less a writer barely 30. Just as sophisticated is her character writing, her insight into relationships, and the fluid articulation of ideas. And along with the insights comes plenty of humor. There's a reason the members of this stellar cast were all drawn to this play. Actors are always looking for great writing, but in this case they're also helping to launch an exciting new writer. And writer and cast alike both depended on the insightful, meticulous direction of Carolyn Cantor to bring this exciting play to life.

> *Tim Sanford*
> *Artistic Director, Playwrights Horizons*

Playwright's Perspective: AMY HERZOG

I had no idea my upbringing was anomalous. In my household, Walt Disney was a villain, Fidel was misunderstood, and the Boy Scouts was a paramilitary organization. I knew the pledge of allegiance represented some mysterious evil before I knew what most of the words in it meant. Communism, far from being a bad word, carried the cozy association of my grandparents' apartment in Greenwich Village where I spent countless weekend afternoons half-listening to the grown-ups' good-natured but voluble political arguments over televised tennis and G&T's.

The blacklist had destroyed my grandfather's burgeoning political career in the fifties, and my extended family was still nursing the wounds of that terrible time. Grandpa had gone on to become a successful businessman (the irony was lost on no one), but he deeply felt the loss of his personal political ambitions and larger ideological aims. As a kid, I strongly identified with my family's left politics; I even felt entitled to my own righteous anger at McCarthy and his reactionary cronies. "My grandfather was blacklisted!" I would announce with great pride and outrage whenever it seemed even tangentially relevant in school or elsewhere. Though his passport was taken away thirty years before I was born, I took my grandfather's political persecution at the hands of our government very personally.

In the spring of 2009, I received a fellowship from the Williamstown Theater Festival to write a play very loosely based on my family, and more broadly about the American Left at the turn of the twenty-first century. By that time, of course, the Soviet Union had long ago dissolved, my grandfather had died, and Morton Sobell had confessed in *The New York Times* that both he and Julius Rosenberg were spies for the Soviet Union.

As I delved into research about the Left in the thirties and forties, I found myself pulled along two opposite poles. On the one hand, I felt longing and envy for the unity of purpose my grandparents experienced in their youth; I felt ashamed of my own generation's relative apathy and lack of idealism. On the other hand, the more I learned about the Soviet Union and the Communist Party, the more I became troubled by my grandparents' dogmatic politics. "There were problems," my grandfather used to say when the subject of Stalin was raised. Intellectually, I can use Marxist political philosophy to justify this shocking understatement. But I can't dispel the discomfort I feel about my grandparents' unshakeable faith in Soviet communism.

Gradually, I realized I was writing a play about disappointment: of parents in their children, children in their parents, siblings and lovers in one another, and adherents in their own belief systems. *After the Revolution* asks how and to what extent we can recover from these disappointments in order to survive as families and to keep fighting for positive change in the world. At the center of the play is the story of a father and daughter whose relationship has largely been built on shared radical politics, until a revelation shatters their close bond. It seems to me that there are far too few father/daughter plays; it's easy to think of plays about fathers and sons, mothers and sons, and to some extent mothers and daughters. Well, of course there's *King Lear* (in which the daughter in question is perfect), *Electra* and *Hedda Gabler* (in which the fathers are dead), and a few others, but there are not many examples of living, flawed fathers and daughters fighting their way to new ground on a shared stage. In the development of the play, I have found that those who are not steeped in recent American history nonetheless relate to the thorny love story between Emma and Ben. After all, for me, politics has always been synonymous with family, and I wrote this play out of love for and frustration with both.

Amy Herzog, August 2010

AMY HERZOG (Playwright) received the 2008 Helen Merrill Award for Aspiring Playwrights. *After the Revolution* was produced on the Nikos Stage at the Williamstown Theatre Festival in summer 2010. Her other plays have been produced at Ensemble Studio Theatre, American Conservatory Theater in San Francisco, The Williamstown Theatre Festival, and the Yale School of Drama; she has had readings and workshops at Manhattan Theatre Club, New York Stage and Film, Arena Stage in Washington, D.C., SoHo Rep, The Rattlestick Playwrights Theater, and The Juilliard School, among others. She performed her solo play, *Love Song in Two Voices*, at the Huntington Theatre/A.R.T.'s "Emerging America" Festival in May 2010. Her play, *4000 Miles*, received readings at Lincoln Center and Steppenwolf in fall 2010. Her short works *508* and *Christmas Present* will be included in forthcoming anthologies published by Applause Books and Vintage. Amy is an alumna of Youngblood and the SoHo RepWriter/Director Lab and the Playwright in Residence at Ars Nova. She holds commissions from The Yale Repertory Theatre, Steppenwolf, and Ars Nova. She teaches Playwriting at Bryn Mawr College. MFA, Yale School of Drama.

PLAYWRIGHTS HORIZONS, celebrating its 40th Anniversary Season, is a writer's theater dedicated to the support and development of contemporary American playwrights, composers and lyricists and to the production of their new work. Under the leadership of Artistic Director Tim Sanford and Managing Director Leslie Marcus, Playwrights Horizons continues to encourage the new work of veteran writers while nurturing an emerging generation of theater artists. Writers are supported through every stage of their growth with a series of development programs: script and score evaluations, commissions, readings, musical theater workshops, Sharp and Mainstage productions. In its 40 years, Playwrights Horizons has presented the work of over 375 writers and is the recipient of numerous awards and honors. Notable productions include four Pulitzer Prize winners—Doug Wright's *I Am My Own Wife* (2004 Tony Award, Best Play), Wendy Wasserstein's *The Heidi Chronicles,* Alfred Uhry's *Driving Miss Daisy* and Stephen Sondheim and James Lapine's *Sunday in the Park With George*—as well as Annie Baker's *Circle Mirror Transformation* (three 2010 Obie Awards, including Best American Play); Doug Wright, Scott Frankel and Michael Korie's *Grey Gardens* (three 2007 Tony Awards); Bruce Norris's *Clybourne Park* and *The Pain and the Itch;* Melissa James Gibson's *This;* Craig Lucas's *Prayer for My Enemy* and *Small Tragedy* (2004 Obie Award, Best American Play); Adam Rapp's *Kindness;* Stephen Sondheim and John Weidman's *Assassins;* Sarah Ruhl's *Dead Man's Cell Phone;* Lynn Nottage's *Fabulation* (2005 Obie Award for Playwriting); Kenneth Lonergan's *Lobby Hero;* David Greenspan's *She Stoops to Comedy* (2003 Obie Award); Kirsten Childs's *The Bubbly Black Girl Sheds Her Chameleon Skin* (2000 Obie Award); Richard Nelson and Shaun Davey's *James Joyce's The Dead;* William Finn's *March of the Falsettos* and *Falsettoland;* Christopher Durang's *Sister Mary Ignatius Explains It All For You* and *Betty's Summer Vacation;* Richard Nelson's *Goodnight Children*

Everywhere and *Franny's Way;* Lynn Ahrens and
Stephen Flaherty's *Once on This Island;* Jon Robin Baitz's
The Substance of Fire; Scott McPherson's *Marvin's Room;*
A.R. Gurney's *Later Life;* Adam Guettel and Tina
Landau's *Floyd Collins;* and Jeanine Tesori and Brian
Crawley's *Violet.* Playwrights Horizons was founded in
1971 by Robert Moss, before moving to 42nd Street where
it has been instrumental in the revitalization of Theatre
Row. André Bishop served as Artistic Director from 1981
to 1991, followed by Don Scardino, who served through
1995. Playwrights' auxiliary programs include the
Playwrights Horizons Theater School, which is affiliated
with NYU's Tisch School of the Arts, and Ticket Central, a
central box office that supports the Off-Broadway
performing arts community.

PLAYWRIGHTS HORIZONS
40 YEARS

FORTY YEARS OF INVENTION. OF DISCOVERY. OF RISK AND REWARD.

Originality has been the hallmark of Playwrights Horizons' work since our first workshop in 1971. From commissions to readings, from first rehearsals to opening nights, "new" has carried the day here. Whether you've come aboard as a ticket buyer, subscriber, donor, artist or volunteer, your presence is an endorsement of our vital mission: **to develop and produce new American theater by the finest emerging and established writers.** That's been our calling for the first forty years, and it will be the driving force that propels the next forty.

40 ANNIVERSARY 1971–2011 SEASON

All photos by Joan Marcus except where noted. Top row: Christine Ebersole in *Grey Gardens*; Deirdre O'Connell in *Circle Mirror Transformation*; Marian Seldes and Brian Murray in *The Butterfly Collection*; LaChanze in *The Bubbly Black Girl Sheds Her Chameleon Skin*. Second row: Crystal A. Dickinson and Damon Gupton in *Clybourne Park*; Blair Brown and Christopher Walken in *James Joyce's The Dead*; Kellie Overbey, Julie Lund, and Kristine Nielsen in *Betty's Summer Vacation*; Tate Donovan and Heather Burns in *Lobby Hero*. Third row: Julie White in *Bad Dates* (photo by Carol Rosegg); Liz Callaway and Phyllis Somerville in *The Spitfire Grill*; Julianne Nicholson in *This*. Bottom row: Alison Fraser and Chip Zien in *March of the Falsettos*.

40 YEARS

PLAYWRIGHTS HORIZONS

of Great American Writers

Noa Ain
Lynn Ahrens
Edward Albee
Fred Alley
Dennis Andersen
Christina Anderson
Dennis Anderson
Billy Aronson
Jon Robin Baitz
Annie Baker
Tanya Barfield
Nathan Barrett
Neal Bell
Adam Bock
Anthony Brazina
E.M. Broner
Keith Bunin
Anne Burr
Rory Butler
David Cale
Craig Carnelia
Lonnie Carter
Michael Carton
Mick Castle
Robert Cesna
Jane Chambers
Kirsten Childs
Julia Cho
Craig Clinton
Bess Coding
Edward M. Cohen
Anne Commire
Tom Cone
Tom Conklin
Kia Corthron
Stephanie Cotsirlos
Randy Courts
Hal Craven
Mike Craver
Brian Crawley
Migdalia Cruz
Shaun Davey
Paul DeJohn
John Dempsey
Donald DiNicola
Ed Dixon
Tom Donaghy
Bathsheba Doran
Marc Dorfmann
Richard Dresser
Christopher Drobny
Mark Dunster

Christopher Durang
Ed DuRante
Susan Dworkin
Mariana Elder
David Epstein
Ron Faber
Sally Fay
Jack Feldman
David Finkle
William Finn
Ellen Fitzhugh
Stephen Flaherty
Kate Fodor
Robert Forrest
Terry Curtis Fox
Scott Frankel
Amy Freed
Eve Friedman
Michael Friedman
Ira Hayes Fuchs
Guy Gauthier
Anthony Giardina
Melissa James
Gibson
William Gill
D. B. Gilles
Tony Giordano
Jessica Goldberg
Daniel Goldfarb
Ricky Ian Gordon
Leslie Gore
Philip Kan Gotanda
David Marshall Grant
Richard Greenberg
David Greenspan
Joy Gregory
Roma Greth
Rinne Groff
Adam Guettel
A.R. Gurney
Harley Hackett
Dennis E. Hackin
Oliver Hailey
Carol Hall
Laura Harrington
Jordan Harrison
Peter Hedges
Kevin Heelan
Jack Heifner
Jack Herrick
Amy Herzog
John Heuser

Paul Hodes
William M. Hoffman
Robert Hogan
Albert Innaurato
Susan Jack
Steven M. Jacobson
Len Jenkin
John Jiler
Tom Johnson
Gus Kaikkonen
Robert Karmon
Barry Keating
Sarah Kernochan
Skip Kennon
Larry Ketron
Frederick Kirwin
Allan Knee
Harry Kondoleon
Michael Korie
Larry Kramer
Jonathan Kreisberg
John B. Kuntz
Christopher Kyle
Michael John
LaChiusa
Tina Landau
John Langs
James Lapine
Peter Larson
Charles Leipart
Ray Leslee
Michael Levenson
Jonathan Levy
John Lewis
Kenneth Lonergan
Quincy Long
Richard Lortz
Dorothy Louise
Craig Lucas
Wendy MacLeod
Gunnar Madsen
Philip Magdalany
Jim Magnuson
Tom Mardirosian
William Marffie
Teresa Marffie
Lynn Martin
Mel Marvin
Marion McClinton
Tom McCormack
Scott McPherson
Ron Melrose

David S. Meranze
Marlane Meyer
Arnold Meyer
Chris Miller
Garrett Morris
Dallas Murphy, Jr.
Jeremiah Murray
Richard Nelson
Maurice Noel
Bruce Norris
Lynn Nottage
Kira Obolensky
Mark O'Donnell
Kevin O'Morrison
Sally Ordway
Eric Overmyer
Peter Parnell
Ralph Pape
Theodore Pappas
Robert Patrick
James Perdeaux
Howard Pflanzer
Richard Ploetz
Regina M. Porter
Margaret Power
Kenneth Pressman
Richard Preston
Adam Rapp
Theresa Rebeck
Keith Reddin
Jonathan Reynolds
Meir Zvi Ribalow
Ronald Ribman
David Rimmer
José Rivera
Lanie Robertson
David Rodgers
Thomas Rosica
Iris Rosofsky
Michael Roth
Charles Rubin
Josh Rubins
Sarah Ruhl
David Rush
James Ryan
Arthur Sainer
Sarah Schulman
David Schumaker
Kathrin King Segal
Bruce Serlen
George Shea
Steven Shea

Jo Ellen Sheffield
Marsha Sheiness
Jonathan Marc
   Sherman
Martin Sherman
Christopher Shinn
Lynn Siefert
Nicky Silver
Evan Smith
Milburn Smith
Beverly Smith-
   Dawson
Stephen Sondheim
Mark St. Germain
James P. Staley
Jim Steinman
Kelly Stuart
Bruce Sussman
Tom Sydorick
Ted Tally
Jay Tarses
Steve Tesich
Jeanine Tesori
Tom Thomas
Eric Thompson
Carl Tiktin
Kathleen Tolan
Tom Topor
David Trainer
Sarah Treem
Karen Trott
Jonathan Tunick
Walter Turney
Nathan Tysen
Yale M. Udoff
Alfred Uhry
Phillip Valcour
James Valcq
Wendy Wasserstein
Daryl Waters
Bill Weeden
John Weidman
George Whitmore
Jack Eric Williams
Erin Cressida Wilson
George C. Wolfe
John Wolfson
Doug Wright
Craig Wright
Stephen Yaffe
Marc Alan Zagoren
Harvey Zuckerman

After the Revolution
By Amy Herzog
Directed by Carolyn Cantor

New York Premiere
Playwrights Horizons
Peter Jay Sharp Theater
Opening Night: November 10, 2010

Cast

Ben .... Peter Friedman
Mel..................... Mare Winningham
Leo .... Mark Blum
Vera .... Lois Smith
Emma .... Katharine Powell
Miguel .... Elliot Villar
Morty.................... David Margulies
Jess................... Meredith Holzman

The play takes place in New York and Boston
in May and June of 1999.

Note: Slashes (/) indicate overlapping dialogue.

This publication represents a draft of *After the
Revolution* as of October 27th, 2010. It does not
reflect changes made during preview performances.

After the Revolution

ACT I

Scene one.
June, 1999

Vera's apartment on West
10th street, early evening
The mood is ebullient, though
everyone is tired

BEN

So it's this program, kids from the projects in Roxbury are
bused out to our school, there's grant money in it for us
and it allows our superintendent to pat herself on the
back but she doesn't actually take / any responsibility for
–

MEL

It's a scandal, it's / really –

BEN

So these kids get a bus ride, but they don't get help
buying textbooks, or paper, they don't get computers –
they're supposed to use our computer lab but then they'd
miss their / bus home –

MEL

And then they're penalized / for –

BEN

And then it's a big surprise they aren't passing their
classes. Our principal calls a meeting, all these kids and
their parents, half the parents don't show, / big surprise –

LEO

Right.

MEL

They're working three jobs, they're gonna come out to the suburbs because their kid's not passing math? I mean this is / their biggest –

LEO

God.

BEN

So the principal is standing up there / *lecturing* –

MEL

This guy is – he should *not* be in education, he has this / punitive –

BEN

The sense is *we are giving your children this opportunity and they are / squandering it* –

MEL

Which is –

BEN

And you can see these parents, the ones who have missed their shift at – Rite Aid or – to be here, they're just glazing over, I mean, they're so / alienated –

MEL

So Ben stands up, / I wish I was there.

BEN

I had been kind of hiding in the – so I stand up and I say my name is Ben Joseph, and I teach history and social justice here, and I'm a Marxist, and I don't think the problem is your children, I think the problem is our society the product of which is this school. I'm sorry that we have failed you, and I want to work with you and your children for change.

MEL

I *wish* I had been there.

                            LEO
And the principal?

                            MEL
Forget / it.

                            BEN
Furious. Goes white. Tries to bring the conversation back
to personal responsibility.

                            MEL
But in the meantime Ben has them working on a list of /
— what was it?

                            BEN
I said this meeting shouldn't be about us telling you what
we need, you should be doing the talking, what do you
need?

                            LEO
Good for you, bro.

                            MEL
What Benji's not telling you is that he told these kids at
the beginning of the year that if they wanted extra help
after school and they missed their bus, he would *drive
them home*, you know, forty-five minutes to – and a lot of
them took him up on it.

                    (brief pause)

                            BEN
And what about you, how were your classes this
semester?

                            LEO
My – I was on sabbatical, I didn't tell you that?

                            BEN
But you didn't travel...?

                                    LEO
Nah, just stayed home to work on the book.

                                    BEN
The same one?

                                    MEL
Don't say it like that.

                                    BEN
Like what? I said / it neutrally.

                                    MEL
It takes a long time to write a book. It takes me a long
time to *read* a book.

                                    LEO
The answer is yes. Same one.
                                    (brief pause)
Sammy's been having a big season, you know, with the
baseball, so it's been good to be around for that, especially
since Beth is working again.

                                    BEN
Well. Standing offer. Trade for a day. Anytime you want
to come in and teach six periods a day I'll do one of your
sociology lectures.

                              (Vera has entered. She is
                              sprightly at eighty-two, but
                              fragile, and maybe a little off
                              balance)
                                    VERA
Has the graduate arrived?

                                    MEL
Not yet.

                                    VERA
What do you think is taking her so long?

BEN

If I know my daughter, she's on the phone with a
journalist, or a / senator –

MEL

She really can't stop working, I think it's a / problem.

BEN

It's not a problem for all the people she's helping, I'll tell
you that.

VERA

Well will somebody come taste my eggplant?

LEO

Your eggplant is perfect, take a load off, join us.

VERA

Well –

MEL

Sit, Vera!

LEO

Here, take my chair.

VERA

I guess I'll allow that.

BEN

We were telling / Leo –

VERA

Louder.

BEN

I was telling my big bro about that meeting, with the
parents / of the –

VERA

Oh, about the black kids.
(to Leo)
Isn't that outrageous, what passes for a, whaddayacallit. /
A social program.

BEN

They're actually – they're about seventy percent African-American, / thirty percent Latino.

VERA

What?

BEN

They're not all black!

(brief pause)

VERA

Who?

(Ben laughs and shakes his head)

LEO
(to Vera)
Doesn't he look more and more like Dad?

MEL
(to Leo)
Oh god, I know, it's uncanny.

BEN

What?

MEL/LEO/VERA

You look like Joe/Dad.
(Leo says 'Dad' where Mel and Vera say 'Joe')

　　　　　　　　　　　　After the Revolution

VERA

And you sound like him. And your politics are like his.
And I think all in all it's pretty wonderful, but that's just
what I think.

(brief pause)

BEN

I was wishing he could've seen Emma up there today.

VERA

Well, he couldn't, and that's that. But then again he also
can't see how all the rest of the grandchildren aren't,
whaddayacallit. In the political scene at all. So maybe
it's for the best.

LEO
(an attempt at light-
heartedness)
Not talking about *my* kids, are you, Vera?

VERA

Yes, I am, I'm talking about Jake, and Katie, and, uh...

LEO

Sammy.

VERA

Right, and all of Janie's kids. They're all very nice people
and so on and so forth, but they're not political. It's not a
criticism, it's just an observation.

LEO

You're my stepmother and I love you but I think it was / a
criticism.

MEL

I've always hated that word, stepmother, I've heard in
French what they say is beautiful mother, now isn't that
nicer?

VERA

What?

BEN

She doesn't like the word stepmother.

MEL

It doesn't do you justice, Vera.

VERA

Oh. Well. You either.

(Emma enters.)

EMMA

Sorry I'm / late.

(Everyone stands, bursts into
applause, cries of Hey!
Brava! Etc.)

Stop it. Stop stop stop. I love you all, now shut up.

BEN

Get over here, kid.

(she goes to her dad, who
bear hugs her)

EMMA

Was it okay?

BEN

Was it okay? Was it *okay?*

EMMA

I couldn't hear myself at all.

(she hugs Mel)

MEL

God I'm proud of you. You know what? Proud is not the right word because that sounds like I did something. I am *glad* for you.

EMMA

Thanks, Mel.

VERA

Emma?

EMMA

I'm really sorry, I was on my way here two hours ago, but Mumia's lawyer called, there's a development in the case and – anyway, sorry.

MEL
(to Vera)
Can you believe the way she just rattles off his first name like that? He's a / celebrity to me.

VERA

Who?

MEL

Mumia Abu Jamal.

BEN

What's the development?

EMMA

And it should have been a five-minute conversation but it never is, with Leonard, hi Uncle Leo, thanks for making it.

LEO

I wouldn't miss it. G&T?

EMMA

No, I feel like I've been drinking for three days straight.

LEO

Why break your streak?

(laughter)

VERA

Emma?

MEL

Do you want to lie down? You know, you don't have to talk to us.

BEN
(laughing)

Yes she does.

VERA
(to Leo)

Did she hear me?

MEL

She's obviously / exhausted! Who wouldn't be?

LEO

Emma!

(Leo points to Vera)

EMMA

I don't need to lie down, I'm fine.
Yes, grandma.

VERA

You could speak a little slower, and restate your point at the end. From the standpoint of propaganda. It was also too long, especially considering the weather.

LEO

Other than that, it was perfect.

(they all laugh)

MEL

It *was* perfect. You are a / born speaker.

BEN

All those privileged white kids, their jaws dropping, like
"did she just call me lazy? At my law school graduation?"
/ Fantastic.

LEO

It was good stuff, Emma. Tough stuff.

VERA

Well excuse me, no one told me that honest criticism was
not allowed.

EMMA

I appreciate your thoughts, grandma.

VERA

It seems to me you're going to make a lot of speeches, over
the course of your – so it's good to learn something, right?
What you said about Joe, and the blacklist, and – it was
wonderful. It was just wonderful and I wish he could've
heard it.

EMMA

Thank you.

MEL

Oh! Maxine.

BEN

Right. Your mom called here. She says big hug, and no
pressure to call but she'll be up late if you can.
                    (to Mel)
Thank you.
                         (with an envelope for Emma)
And this is from Jane.

MEL

From Jane and Peter.

BEN

From – from my sister and that guy she married, right.

EMMA
(to everyone)

You guys really didn't think it was too aggressive? My speech?

BEN

No.

LEO

You walked a line.

EMMA

Is that a yes, Uncle Leo?

LEO
(equivocally)

Uh, no, it's not.

BEN

You can't fight for change and be a nice guy, you can't / have both.

MEL

It was bracing. That's the word I've been looking for.

EMMA
(with the contents of the
envelope)

Oh my God.

MEL

She just made the whole thing out to you, so you can give half to the fund and keep half, or whatever, whatever you want, but she insists you keep at least a little bit for yourself.

                            BEN
I told her, fat chance.

                            EMMA
This is so generous.

                            LEO
That's Janie for / you.

                            VERA
From Jane?

                            MEL
From Jane and / Peter.

                            VERA
Well, they make a lot of money.

                            MEL
Is anyone else starving?

                            LEO
I'm getting hungry, / yeah.

                            BEN
We're still waiting for one, right?

                            EMMA
Oh! No, we're not.

                            MEL
What? He's not coming?

                            EMMA
Sorry, we both had so many graduation parties, we decided to split them up.

MEL

Well that's a big big bummer.

VERA

What's / the problem?

LEO

The real question is, did his family get to meet you?

(brief pause)

EVERYONE BUT EMMA

Oh!, okay, etc.

EMMA

Okay, his family didn't cross examine me about my opinions vis a vis Fidel, Palestine, / affirmative action –

BEN

How did you end up such a high functioning, socially acceptable young woman, coming from / this family?

EMMA

I ask myself that every day, dad, / literally.

MEL

If you're with him I'm sure he has great politics.

EMMA

Good politics in my generation is different from good politics in your / generation, Mel.

MEL

We understand that, we're not dinosaurs, we're not Stalin apologists.

VERA

What? What about Stalin?

After the Revolution

EMMA

You'll get to meet him / eventually.

LEO

Maybe he wants to come to the family reunion in August.

(general chorus of
oooohhhhhhs and laughter)

EMMA

Don't count on it.

VERA

I can't hear a word any of you is saying. Or maybe that
was the point.

(The phone rings. Vera
considers getting up.)

MEL

I'll get it.

(Mel exits)

EMMA
(loudly)

We're talking about my boyfriend, grandma. I told you
about him, he's going to be working with me this year, on
the fund.

LEO

I didn't know that. Not worried about mixing work and
play?

BEN

A lot of great political couples worked together.

EMMA

We're not a "great political couple," dad, let's keep the vicarious delusions of grandeur to some kind of /
minimum.

VERA

What's his name again?

EMMA

Miguel.

VERA

What?

EMMA

/Miguel.

BEN
(in his best Spanish accent)

Miguel Roja, de Puerto Rico.

EMMA

Dad.

VERA

What was the last one's name?

EMMA
(brief pause)

Carlos.

(Vera raises her eyebrows
slightly but declines to
comment. Mel reenters)

MEL

Leo, Beth for you.
(to everyone)
She's sorry to interrupt the celebration.

                              LEO
                          (on his way out)
She okay?

                          (Mel shrugs and nods; he
                          exits)

                              BEN
Well, before we adjourn to the dining room.
                          (picks up his glass)

                              MEL
Honey, I support everything you're about to say and just
want to remind you that we're all really hungry.
                              BEN
I'll keep it short.
Emma.

                          (brief pause)

                              EMMA
Do not cry, dad, no crying; you'll make me cry.

                              BEN
Arright arright. As your father, and therefore a totally
impartial, / objective –
                          (interjections of uh-huh,
                          right, etc.)
Shit, Emma, it's 1999. In this decade we saw the Soviet
Union collapse and my dad die. Clinton is a big business
president, the poor are getting poorer, racial divides are
deepening, we're dropping bombs in the Balkans, and
people are complacent. We're about to see a new
millennium and it's hard to imagine things getting much
worse.

                              VERA
That's a fact.

                        BEN

But...

                       EMMA

No crying!

                        BEN

Okay! *But.* A handful of things make me feel hopeful,
and top of the list, no question: you, standing up there
today, speaking for Mumia, for dad, and I know we
disagree about this word, but I'd say for revolution. And
so I want to raise a glass and say not congratulations but
thank you.

                        MEL

Hear hear.

                              ("To Emma" "cheers," etc.
                              Leo reenters, shaken)

                        BEN

And I didn't cry! And let's eat!

                        LEO

Benny?

                       EMMA

Thanks, Dad.

                        BEN

No no, that's the point. Thank *you.*

                        LEO

Ben.

                        BEN

What? I'm hungry, come on!

                              (Leo follows him off)

                    VERA
Well, not in my lifetime.

                    MEL
What not in your lifetime, Vera?

                    VERA
Everything. What we were fighting for.
                    (to Emma)
Maybe in yours.
                    (end scene)

After the Revolution

                    Scene two.
                    The kitchen, a few hours
                    later.
                    Ben sits with his head in his
                    hands. Leo stands.

                         LEO
The good news is, we have some advance notice. If I
didn't have this friend at Yale Press, the book would have
come out, she would have been blindsided.

                         BEN
Shit. Shit shit shit.

                         LEO
This gives us a couple of weeks.

                         BEN
I honestly never believed this would happen. Those
fucking bastards.

                         LEO
Agreed, but let's not dwell on that when we need to be
making a plan.

                         BEN
Actually I would like to dwell on it for just a minute, it's
dad, it's dad's name.

                         LEO
And Emma has been invoking Dad's name publicly for the
last four years and there are gonna be some consequences,
I'm not sure if you understand / the depth of –

                         BEN
I understand, it's gonna kill her, I understand very well.
                    (Mel enters, perturbed)

MEL

Shit, her hearing's gotten so much worse. I needed a
break. I wish I believed in God and thought there was
some fucking good reason for us all to go deaf blind and
incontinent eventually.
Where's Emma?

LEO

She said she needed some air, which I know from my kids
is code for smoking a cigarette.

MEL/ BEN

Emma doesn't smoke.
                         (brief pause)

MEL

What's going on in here?

LEO

We're sort of in the middle of something.

MEL

Benji?

BEN

I'm okay. Can you give us a minute?

MEL

Yeah, and then I'd like you to tell me what's going on.
                         (she exits)

LEO

You should tell Emma in person, while we're in New York.

BEN

Obviously!

LEO

Okay, why don't you tell me how I can be helpful to you
right now.

BEN

You could show a little outrage! A little indignation!

LEO

Uh...

BEN

Or is that too much to ask?

(pause)

LEO

Up to you, okay? But if you want me to be there when you tell her, I will.

Scene three.
Emma's apartment, late that
night. Emma and Miguel
mid-conversation.

MIGUEL

Your mom didn't make it?

EMMA

Are you kidding? She has chronic migraines, and gas is
expensive, and…it's Monday…so. Of course not. Mel
asked for your address so that she can send you her
monthly newsletter about responsible consumerism
(sorry). And my dad wanted me to convey to you a
greeting in Spanish but I refused. He says
congratulations on graduating.

MIGUEL

His Spanish is probably better than mine.

EMMA

His Spanish is most definitely *not* better than — what is
that? No!

(he has produced a wrapped
item)

MIGUEL

Just a little –

EMMA

We agreed!

MIGUEL

It didn't really cost anything.

EMMA

I didn't know *free* presents were allowed!

MIGUEL

Will you please open it?

EMMA

I feel very betrayed.

> (she opens it. It's a framed picture.
> She is moved.)

MIGUEL

For our new office.

EMMA

Miguel.

MIGUEL

Because I didn't think the décor should be left up to you, no offense. And I thought he should be up there.

EMMA

Where did you get it?

MIGUEL

You can just write in to the Times, they have this archive, they'll send you a print of any – because it's what they ran when he testified.

EMMA

It's so weird to see him without his glasses, especially toward the end he had these thick, like magnifying glasses on his...he just looks so vulnerable.

MIGUEL

If you don't like it.

EMMA

No –

MIGUEL

Because I know, it memorializes like the worst day in his
life, but I thought it would be good, to – you know, to
honor that.
But I completely understand if you –

EMMA

I love it.
                    (she kisses him.)
I can't wait to tell my dad and Mel you did this.
                    (off his look)
What?

MIGUEL

Nothing, I just. I want to meet them.

EMMA

I know. I want you to meet them too.

MIGUEL

So...?

EMMA

So I'm just picturing my dad wearing his Che T-shirt in
preparation and Mel saying over and over that you have
an amazing *face* and I know you'll rise above it but I'll be
humiliated, that's all.

MIGUEL

What will I rise above?

EMMA

Seriously?

MIGUEL

Yeah.

EMMA

Um, the insidious brand of leftist racism in my family?

MIGUEL

You're saying they're going to be welcoming to me.

EMMA

That is understatement.

MIGUEL

And I should take that to be racist.

(pause)

EMMA

Do you think *I'm* being racist?

MIGUEL

I think you're throwing that word around in a way that makes me uncomfortable.

EMMA

I'm just so surprised you haven't remarked on this kind of thing before.

MIGUEL

If every time a white person was nice to me, I thought it was racism? I'd lead a pretty dark life, Emma.
                    (brief pause. Off her look of
                    concern)
Hey, stay with me.

EMMA

Sorry. I've just been fighting off the feeling all day that lunch with your parents was like an unmitigated disaster and you haven't said anything about it yet, so...

MIGUEL

What? No, no...

EMMA

Tell me the truth.

MIGUEL

The restaurant was loud, it was hard to hear each other.

EMMA

And they basically never said a word, so I was essentially yelling across the table for an hour and a half about – I don't even know what about.

MIGUEL

I told you they're shy at first.

EMMA

Yeah, but...

MIGUEL

What?

EMMA

You could've helped me out. I mean, you were like...silent...Sid over there.

MIGUEL

Silent / Sid?

EMMA

Why weren't you talking?

MIGUEL

I – I don't know, I just felt...kinda down – my parents were – I think they thought it was gonna be some kinda corny culmination of immigrant dreams, you know, Oldest Son Graduates from Top Law school, and it was cold, and boring, and their camera ran out of batteries, and...I told you they're not totally thrilled about me taking this job.

EMMA

No you didn't.

MIGUEL

I didn't? Oh. Well – it's not anything you should worry
about, but from their perspective, it's like, I took out all
these loans and now I'm making thirty-thousand dollars a
year working for my gringa girlfriend.

(pause)

EMMA

Ouch.

MIGUEL

But I don't want you to worry about it.

EMMA

Oh sure, absolutely, I'll just put it completely out of my
mind.

MIGUEL

Emma.

EMMA

No, that makes me feel terrible, of course it does.

MIGUEL

Well it's not up to them. I'm doing what I believe in.
Three years ago I didn't know what I believed in, now I
do. If they can't be proud of that, that's their problem.

(brief pause)

EMMA

So I guess it wasn't the smoothest move on my part to
monologue endlessly about the fund.

MIGUEL

Oh – also, with my dad's business, he's pretty tight with
the local police, so the fact that our primary goal is to
exonerate an accused cop killer...that's like the icing on
the shit cake.

EMMA

Miguel!

MIGUEL

What?

EMMA

You have to tell me these things! I'm awesome with parents, that's like one of my primary characteristics, I can't believe you let me fuck that up.

MIGUEL

We'll go out to New Brunswick, spend the night, they'll get to know you and they'll love you.

EMMA

So it *was* a disaster.

MIGUEL

No! No.
Hey, at least you got to meet mine.

(pause)

EMMA

I'm going to see my dad tomorrow before he goes back to Boston, and I'd invite you, / but –

MIGUEL

Right, right.

EMMA

No, but he says he has something quote unquote important to tell me, it doesn't seem like an ideal moment.

MIGUEL

What do you think it is?

EMMA

I'm sure it's about Jess. I know this makes me a terrible sister, but I just don't have the energy anymore, if she's back in rehab I don't know why he can't tell me that on the phone. Do I sound callous?

MIGUEL

Yes.

EMMA

I'm just ready for her to stop torturing my dad; she's put him through so much.
Listen, be patient with me, it's just…if you didn't absolutely love him, that would be hard for me to have a sense of humor about.

MIGUEL

Noted. Hey.

EMMA

Hm?

MIGUEL

I'm excited to see you at work tomorrow.

EMMA

You're not staying over?

MIGUEL

I'm staying over. I'm just saying.

> (She pulls away from him
> testily, he pulls her back and
> kisses her. She relaxes into
> it. It goes on)

Scene four

The next day. Leo, Ben and
Emma in the apartment on
W. 10th street. Pause.

BEN

Uhhhhh.

LEO

Take your time.

EMMA

What's going on?

LEO

Give him a minute.

EMMA

Okay you're freaking me out.

LEO

It's okay. He just needs a little time.

EMMA

Well I have a meeting with a major donor / in half –

LEO

You're going to be late. Sit down.

(she does)

EMMA

...dad?
Is this about – are you okay?

BEN

I'm okay.

EMMA

Jess?

BEN

Your sister's fine. She's the same. Mel's fine –

EMMA

Then — ?

LEO

He's getting there.

> (Ben looks at Leo, who nods
> encouragingly)

BEN

In your, uh. Research, or in class. Did you ever come
across the word Venona?

EMMA

I don't know, rings a distant bell.

BEN

Soviet cables, between the US and Russia during World
War II. Some people got lazy, reused pages from the code
book, it allowed American intelligence to decrypt some
thousands of cables. This was known as the Venona
project.

EMMA

Okay, yes, vaguely.

LEO

A few years ago a lot of this information was declassified.
You may remember that the Rosenbergs –

BEN

Can we leave the Rosenbergs out of it?

LEO

I was just giving / her some context.

BEN

I don't like that context.

EMMA

I do remember, there was evidence of Julius Rosenberg's guilt, maybe, or maybe it was bullshit. I'm sorry, where is this going?

(pause)

BEN

There's a book coming out, it'll be in stores soon. It uses the Venona source material to name American spies for the Soviet Union in the forties.

EMMA

Okay...
And?

(Ben looking down)

LEO

Dad was named. He has a two-page entry.

(long pause)

EMMA

Okay. Wow, that is – *wow*. So what's our strategy?

LEO

What do you mean?

EMMA

How do we fight it? We should issue a statement before it's reviewed. Have you been in touch with family members of other people who were named – or even better, are some of them still living?

LEO

Uh –

EMMA

We need to *move* on this, it's fifty years later and / they're
still –

LEO

Emma, hold on.

BEN

She's right, it's exactly what I've / been –

LEO

She doesn't understand yet.

EMMA

What don't I understand?

>   (Leo looks at Ben who doesn't
>   pick up the thread)

LEO

We're not going to contest it. First of all, it's two pages in
a five-hundred page book that almost no one is going to
read. If it weren't for your work, for the likelihood
someone will call your attention to it, we might not even
be having this conversation.

EMMA

And second of all?

LEO

Benny.

EMMA

Dad?

>   (pause)

BEN

Look, I haven't read the copy, it could be total fucking
James Bond fabricated BS.

LEO

Except that it's not.

BEN

You haven't read it either. You're just willing to accept /
what some right wing –

LEO

Because we know it's true.

BEN

Not the particulars.

LEO

Not the particulars, no. But the essence of it.

BEN

I disagree; I think it's the essence they have one hundred /
percent misconstrued.

LEO

Not having read it.

EMMA

One of you really has to tell me what's going on.

LEO

I'm going to get a glass of water.
                    (Leo exits)

BEN

You know the history, I don't have to tell you that Russia
was our ally in / World War II.

EMMA

Dad.

BEN

That Russian men and women were dying by the millions
to fight fascism and we repaid them with stingy
intelligence, by freezing them out of / the major –

EMMA

Stop stop stop.

BEN

Look, Leo would have it that we know something
definitive about what happened during those years, but
the truth is we weren't born yet and what Dad said to us
about it was along the lines of "We did what we had to
do." I don't think that's as conclusive as my brother
seems to.

(brief pause)

EMMA

You told me – you've always told me. That grandpa Joe
was blacklisted because he was an ideological communist.
That's what I've been standing at podiums and repeating
for the last four years.

BEN

And it's true, I firmly believe that is why he was
blacklisted.

EMMA

But you're telling me something different now.

BEN

Well –

EMMA

Dad. When grandpa said "We did what we had to do."
What did you think that meant, at the time?

BEN

Uh. In the context, which I don't remember that clearly.
It seemed to mean that he passed information to Soviet
Agents during World War II.

(pause)

EMMA

Did you ever think about telling me?

BEN

Yes. Often.

EMMA

Why didn't you?

(Leo reenters. A pause.)

LEO

So this is gonna create some awkwardness for you.

EMMA

Yeah.

LEO

What you need to keep in mind: however ugly it gets these next few weeks, no one will remember in a year. You just have to ride it out. The work you do is still terrific. It's still true he was blacklisted, that's still persecution and it shouldn't have happened.

EMMA

No, he shouldn't have been blacklisted.
He should have been tried for espionage.

BEN

Emma.

EMMA
(to Leo)

Ride it out? The whole thing is predicated on his innocence; the fund is *named* after him.

LEO

That's maybe something you'll have to look at.

BEN

What?

EMMA

Mumia's detractors are going to have a fucking field day
with / this, oh god, oh god, –

BEN

You're telling her to rename the fund?

LEO

No, but it's something she may have to consider.

BEN

Emma, no, you do not bow down to these fuckers, you
don't do that.

LEO

It's not about bowing down or not bowing down, it's what's
politically expedient.

EMMA
(to Leo)

I have to think about the consequences for Mumia, for all
the people I've bound up in / Joe's reputation.

LEO

Okay, but take it one step at a / time.

BEN

You're a Marxist, Emma, you educate. You use your
platform to explain what these bastards are doing, that
it's McCarthy rearing his head, that your grandfather
dared to question the powerful and he's dead now and
they're still not done punishing him.

EMMA
(all icy rage)
Dad. You sacrificed your chance to be part of this
conversation when you lied to me for my whole life.
Please stay out of it.

> (pause. A stunned, hurt Ben
> returns her iciness)

BEN
Well maybe you can see why I didn't tell you, the way
you're dealing with this. I guess I was right to wonder
whether you'd do the right thing.

> (pause. Emma gets her bag.)

LEO
Let's not leave it like that.

EMMA
I have a meeting.

LEO
Let's finish the conversation.

EMMA
I have nothing more to say.

> (She exits.)

Scene five.

Morty and Emma at a table
at Gene's restaurant in the
village; Emma has just
arrived. Two glasses of
champagne are on the table.

MORTY

I'm very happy that we're meeting today because today is
a special anniversary for me. Today I have lived in
Greenwich Village for sixty years.

EMMA

...wow.

MORTY

I moved to Greenwich Village from the Bronx when I was
seventeen years old and I never left. Even once I made
enough money to leave, I didn't want to.

EMMA

Well happy anniversary. I'm so sorry to have kept you
waiting, / I was –

MORTY

You're busy, I understand. I was busy once too, I can
faintly remember. Now that you're done with school, just
having the one job will seem like vacation, right?

EMMA

Um –

MORTY

I'm teasing you, I know you'll just work twice as hard.
How is your beautiful grandmother?

EMMA

She's well. I mean, she still misses Joe a lot, so...

MORTY

No disrespect to your grandfather, who I greatly admired,
but as soon as she is fully recovered I hope she will go on
a date with me.

(Emma laughs awkwardly)

I saw her at the tennis courts in Central Park a few weeks
ago, playing doubles. I told her she should call me if they
were ever short a player, she said she didn't think she
would. Just like that, she said, "I don't think I'll do that,
Morty." I like a woman who's honest.

EMMA

Now I'd hate to think your generosity to the fund has
anything to do with getting a date with my grandmother.

MORTY

Absolutely not; of course not.
Now if my generosity to your fund resulted in a date with
your grandmother, I would not refuse on principle. But I
have no expectations – none.
Now before I forget, last night I'm having dinner with
some friends, and we're talking about which organizations
we give money to, which is a way old lefties show off and
pass the time and put off thoughts of death. I say, more
and more I give to just one organization, the Joe Joseph
fund. My friend, who is to say the least a financially
comfortable individual, he says, I know of that fund, and
I'm very impressed with the young lady who runs it, et
cetera, but I've reviewed the facts, and that Mumia Abu-
Jamal, I just don't think he's innocent. I said, well first of
all you're wrong, second of all you've missed the point, the
question is not simply did he shoot the cop or didn't he,
it's did he receive a fair trial, was he set up, would he be
on Death Row if he wasn't a Black Panther? I said have
you forgotten the lessons of McCarthyism? We have to
stand up when people are persecuted for their political
affiliations. So how did I do?

EMMA

You did great, Morty, I'm afraid I've created a monster

MORTY

Well my friend wasn't convinced. Here is his name and
telephone number. He's a pain in the ass, good luck
getting two words in, but you're more persuasive than I
am, not to mention better looking, and if you can get him
to come around he's good for ten-thousand a year, easy.

EMMA

Thanks.

MORTY

I do what I can. I took the liberty of ordering champagne.
Nothing is too good for the proletariat, right?

(he lifts a glass)

EMMA
(gently scolding)

Morty...

MORTY

Admittedly an extravagance at lunch, but you just
graduated and I'll turn up my toes soon and everything I
don't spend will be taxed to hell anyway.
To the most extraordinary young woman I know, who has
given me something to live for in my decrepit old age.

EMMA
(they drink)

You're not really that old, Morty.

MORTY

I'm six years younger than your grandmother; that's what
you're thinking. But I don't think age should stand in the
way of true love.

EMMA

I'm thinking that you have a lot of years ahead of you and you should act like it.

MORTY

Well that's a good segue to what I want to talk to you about.

EMMA

First / I–

MORTY

And I don't want any objections, I don't want a fuss, I thought about not telling you, but it was an excuse to have lunch with you and anyway you should know because it will help you plan for the future.

EMMA

You're scaring me, a little.

MORTY

It's very simple. I'm leaving everything to your fund. All of it; everything; the whole kit and kaboodle.
                    (off her look)
Now I said no fuss.

EMMA

But –

MORTY

That's all. My accountant will be in touch with you to give you an idea of the figures. You and I never need to talk about it again.

EMMA

I can't –

MORTY

Yes you can.

EMMA

Morty –

MORTY

Yes. You can.

EMMA

I have to tell you why this incredibly generous offer
makes me feel so anxious / right now.

MORTY

Listen, I know. I knew you'd bring up my children,
because I know how you feel about family. They're all
right. They all make a good living at this point, with the
exception of Kathy, who – well, never mind about Kathy.
And I've given them plenty of help along the way. Now
I'm not saying it will be easy to explain to them –

EMMA
(forcefully)

But you have to, you have to explain it to them.

MORTY

I understand.

EMMA

You can't just let them find out after you're gone, Morty,
you have to tell them.

(she has gotten quite upset)

MORTY
(gently)

Okay, okay, that's all right. I'm sorry I upset you.
But I want you to listen to an old man on a soapbox for
just a minute.
I was around when what happened to your
grandfather...happened. I was what they called a fellow
traveler, which meant I was never a member of the party
but I was known to be sympathetic to those who were.

Until things got really hairy, and then I kept my distance.
From good friends who could have used my help, I kept
my distance. Do you know, Emma, that to this day I
thank god that I was never asked to appear and name
names, because I'm almost sure I would have done it?

EMMA

You don't know that.

MORTY

It's my best guess. Men like your grandfather...
Who took the fifth, who took the consequences.
You are a young person with the courage of your
convictions. It is my greatest and last honor to help you.
Now what was it you wanted to tell me?

(End scene)

Scene six.

Ben on Emma's answering
machine.

BEN

Hi! Hey, sweetie. About our talk the other day…I'm
sorry about how it went, and let's not have this silence,
okay? It's eating me up and I think it's probably eating
you up too. I know you have some big decisions to make.
I want to be part of that. I think I have a right to be a
part of that. And I don't want you to do something you'll
regret later.

I thought you'd appreciate this, though, last day of classes
before finals today, one of my sophomores, I think I told
you about him, one of my Roxbury kids, never spoke in
class, one of those kids with the jeans below his ass and
the big hood with the baby face under it. This afternoon
came up and thanked me for a good year. Told me he now
considers himself a Marxist. *Not* what I imagined he was
thinking all that time I was up front bloviating and he
was carving shit into his desk.

So. I got one.

And I'm waiting for your call.

After the Revolution

Scene Seven.

Emma and Vera, in the apartment in New York, having just finished eating.

VERA

So this new fella.

EMMA

Miguel.

VERA

Miguel. It's serious.

EMMA

We've been together since September.

VERA

Right. But is it serious?

EMMA

I…guess I don't know what people mean when they say that. I wouldn't still be with him if I didn't take him seriously.
                              (Vera chews, watching her)
What?

VERA

Didn't say anything.

EMMA

What, grandma?

VERA

I think you should be honest with him, that's all. Because I don't think you're serious, and it sounds to me like he is. That's all.
                              (pause. They eat.)

Have I told you about the lesbian who tried to seduce /
me?

Yes.

She showed up at the house, saying she had such a big,
whaddayacallit.

EMMA
Clitoris.

VERA
Clitoris, right, and she said it would be terrific, and all
that. And I said no thank you, and she went away. Nice
woman. Very pretty, actually. But she had been, um.
Whaddayacallit.

EMMA
(reluctantly, but she knows every word of this story)
Sexually / abused.

VERA
Sexually abused, right.
                    (brief pause)
Which most of them / have been.

EMMA
Oh grandma, that's *not true*.

VERA
Well. I'm not saying all of them.
But almost all of them.

EMMA
I could show you studies, it's not true.

VERA
All right, all right. I'm only saying, from my experience.

EMMA

This is all to say...?

VERA

What?

EMMA

What's your point?
You went from asking about Miguel to telling / your old
lesbian classic.

VERA

Oh, because. You know your father hoped you would be a
lesbian. You or your sister. Which I always thought was
pretty strange.

EMMA

It's not that he / hoped one –

VERA

You have to talk louder if you want me to hear.

EMMA

It's not that he hoped we would be gay, it's that he wanted
to create the space in – I still don't understand the
connection.

VERA

I'm saying, just because your father wanted you to be gay,
and you're not. Doesn't mean you have to go out with the
kind of guys you always go out with.
                    (pause)
It's all right if you want to. It doesn't bother me. I just
don't think you need to have a rule about it, to please your
father.

EMMA

I don't have a rule about it. The last two *happened* to be
Latino.

VERA

I think the fact that you're so sensitive about it, that's
something you should look into.
(pause)
And I've never understood your prejudice against Jewish
men.

EMMA

I do not have a prejudice / against Jewish men!

VERA

I mean you'll do what you want, you always have, but you
should just think about what you could be missing in
terms of a, whaddayacallit, a common, a love of, of, books,
and thinking about the important things, and an easy
way of talking to each other. That's all.

EMMA

Well, Miguel loves books, and he thinks about important
things, and we have an easy way of talking to each other.
And I hoped we could talk about Grandpa Joe.
(brief pause)

VERA

Sure. We can talk about Joe.

EMMA

I'm not sure how much my dad told you / about –

VERA

He told me about that filthy book, I know all about it. It's
the first time in a year and a half I've been glad Joe is
gone, so he never had to see that. Disgusting, Emma. It's
just disgusting.

EMMA

I want to ask you about Joe's activities. In the forties.

VERA

We weren't married in the forties.

EMMA

I know that.

VERA

We were married in nineteen fifty-eight.

EMMA

I know, grandma, but he must have told you about that time, when he was working for the Office of Strategic Services.

VERA

That was during the war.

EMMA

Right. He was an economist in the Japanese Division.

VERA

Well, he was a brilliant man. Did you know he had just been appointed special assistant to Trygvie Lie when they took his passport away in '49? That was when the UN was just really getting started, and he was a big part of it. He was supposed to have a brilliant political career, that's what was supposed to happen. Do you want dessert? I have some delicious plums.

EMMA

Thanks, I'm full.

VERA
(exiting)

They're very small.

(Vera exits. She returns a moment later with plums)

What?

EMMA

What?

VERA

What did you say?

EMMA

I didn't say anything.

VERA
                    (embarrassed and frustrated)
You know, my hearing really isn't very good. I can't find
words anymore, either.. I say "whaddayacallit" all the
time, I sound like a dummy.

EMMA

No you don't.

VERA

Don't get old, Emma.
Now isn't that delicious?

EMMA

It is.
Grandma, I didn't know until a few days ago that
Grandpa was a spy.
                    (Vera stiffens)
I'm hoping you can help me understand better what he
did, and why he did it.
                    (pause)

VERA

Well. I'm not a rah-rah American. So.
                    (brief pause)

EMMA

What does that mean?

VERA

Just that I'm not a rah-rah American. If I were a rah-rah
American I would see it one way, but I'm not, so I don't.

                          EMMA

I don't think you have to be a rah-rah American to
question the ethics of spying.

                          VERA

That word again.

                          EMMA

He passed government secrets to Soviet Agents, / what
else should I call it?

                          VERA

Listen, Joe was a member of the communist party, you
know that. Anybody with a beating heart and a half a
brain was back then, that's hard for people to understand
nowadays, because people have become
so...whaddayacallit. Apathetic. But it's true. And the
Russians were really the ones fighting the war, not us,
and some people were very happy to sit back and let them
die, even some people in the party, and some people like
your grandfather were not.   You're talking about ethics,
well those were his ethics, not to turn his back on his
comrades who were fighting fascism.

                          EMMA

So you're saying his allegiance wasn't to the self-
interested US government.

                          VERA

Right!

                          EMMA

It was to Stalin.
                          (brief pause)

                          VERA
                       (flummoxed)
Listen, you – he – a lot of what you hear about Stalin in
this country is propaganda, it's / not –

EMMA

Oh, Grandma!

VERA

There were a lot of wonderful things about the Soviet
Union! The papers would never report that because they
didn't want the American people to know the / truth.

EMMA

Vera, / you can't –

VERA

And whatever else you want to say the fact remains that
it was really Stalin and the Russians who were stopping
Hitler from killing all the Jews!

EMMA

Stalin was slaughtering Jews in his own country, and
homosexuals, and / dissidents.

VERA

Well we didn't know that then!
And I still don't know how much of all that is true.
(pause)

EMMA

I should tell you that I'm thinking of making a public
statement about this before the book comes out.

VERA

What?

EMMA
(loudly)

I may / make a –

VERA

I heard you.

What kind of public statement? The kind where you
defend your grandfather against those bullies? That's
what I hope you mean, Emma Joseph.

EMMA

It may not be as simple as that.

VERA

Well the question is which side are you on, that's the
question.

(brief pause)

EMMA

Thank you for your time.
(she stands with some dishes)

VERA

Leave those.

EMMA

I'll just put them / in the dishwasher.

VERA

I said *leave them*!

(Emma reacts. End scene.)

After the Revolution

JESS

And he's cool about working for you?

EMMA

What do you mean?

JESS

A lot of guys couldn't handle that.

EMMA

He's a feminist.

JESS

Yeah, he's dating you, it goes without saying he's a
feminist, but...

EMMA

What?

JESS

No, if it's working, it's working. I mean, *I* would not want
to be your employee, I give him a lot of credit.
>   (Emma bristles slightly at
>   this)
I'm kidding! I'm teasing you!

EMMA

I know.
>   (brief pause)
What about you? New man in your life?

JESS

No, my year's not quite up yet.

EMMA

Your — ?

JESS

Oh. You're not supposed to date anyone until you've been
out for at least a year.

EMMA

Oh. Oh.

JESS

No need to be embarrassed.

EMMA

I'm not.

JESS

You are, but it's cool.
                              (brief pause)
Mel said your speech was incredible.

EMMA

You talked to Mel?

JESS

We talk on Sundays.   Sometimes dad gets on the phone,
if he's not feeling too emotionally fragile. Which he was
this week.

EMMA

Are you serious? He won't get on the phone with you?

JESS

Not out of malice, he just – you know him, he gets upset.

EMMA

I just think that's incredibly fucked up.

JESS

Whoa, negative words about our father?

EMMA

I'm shocked.

JESS

Well. It's not like you're calling me every Sunday, sis.

EMMA

I'm sorry.

JESS

Yeah, let's not do that, I'm just making the point that it can be a challenge to have an addict in the family, I'm done throwing the blame around.

EMMA
(the sarcasm slips out)

That's clear.

(brief pause)

JESS

What?

(Emma shakes her head)

EMMA

So I actually need to tell you something.

JESS

Yeah, I thought it was a long trip just for a visit.

EMMA

This going to be really hard. But I was very hurt that no one told me, and I made it a priority to come tell you in person.

JESS

Okay. I'm listening.

EMMA

Grandpa Joe spied for the Russians during World War II.

(Pause. No discernible
reaction from Jess)

JESS

I'm just thinking about how to respond to this.

EMMA

I know. I know.

JESS

No, um. I don't think you do. Actually.
Sweetie, I already knew that.
Should I not have told you that?

EMMA
(forced calm)

How did you know?

JESS

Dad told me.

(brief pause)

EMMA

When?

JESS

When? Um. Three? No four. Four? Years ago?

EMMA

Four *years* ago?

JESS

It was right after the first time I got out of rehab, so that
was...ninety-five. Yeah, about four years ago.

EMMA

How did it.../come up?

JESS

Funny story, actually. It was when he took me on that trip to London, that 'you got out of rehab' reward, penitent-father-fucked-up-daughter-bonding-type-thing. And while we were there he took me to Marx's grave. Not first on my list of tourist attractions but also not up for debate. And he started crying. Which I found to be over the top. I asked him what was wrong, and that's when he told me.

EMMA

He said grandpa was a spy.

JESS

That was the gist of it. And I was kind of like, I appreciate your sharing this huge thing with me, but we both know the real reason you're crying is that I'm such a colossal disappointment so let's not dress it up, you know?

EMMA

1995 was the year I started the Joe Joseph fund.

JESS

Okay.

EMMA

It just seems like it might have come up.

JESS

I was back in rehab three weeks later, so it wasn't strictly speaking my tip-top priority.

EMMA

Well I guess that's the end of the conversation.

JESS

What does that mean?

EMMA

That's how you avoid every tough subject, that's how you
recuse yourself from being part of our family, I'm not sure
if you're aware of that.

JESS

He specifically asked me not to tell you. That's why I
didn't say anything.
I'm sorry you put me in a position where I had to tell you
that.
                    (brief pause)
You know in group I talk about you a lot. About how I
feel bad that you didn't really get to have a childhood,
fucked up as I was.

EMMA

I'm sorry, but I'm not sure what the right response is to
that. Is it thank you?

                         (pause. Jess takes this with
                         some grace.)

JESS

Are you staying with Dad and Mel, while you're up here?

EMMA

No. With Uncle Leo.

JESS

Can I give you one tiny piece of advice?   Punishing dad
isn't as fun or satisfying as you think it's going to be.

EMMA

I'm not punishing him.

JESS

Okay.

EMMA

I'm trying to surround the situation.

JESS

Well go easy on him.

EMMA

Are you *serious*?

JESS

The irony is not lost on me. Just some hard won wisdom,
or whatever.

(brief pause)

You gonna be okay?

EMMA

Am *I* gonna be okay?

JESS

Um. Yeah.

(they look at each other. End
scene.)

Scene nine.

Emma at Leo's house in the middle of the night. She sits at a table, drinking tea, poring over a document.

Leo enters in his pajamas.

LEO

Sammy get home?

(she startles)

Sorry.

EMMA

Yeah, a while ago. He made curfew.

LEO

Good. Sober?

EMMA
(lying)

What? I think so.

LEO
(he's not buying it)

Good cousin.

(she averts his gaze)

EMMA

Katie's so grown up.

LEO

She's somethin', huh?

EMMA

She – while you and Beth were cooking she asked what I was doing in Boston and I started to tell her –

LEO

Oh.

EMMA

But I realized you – so I didn't say anything.

LEO

Thanks.

EMMA

But you should tell her.

LEO

Keep meaning to. Somehow it...

EMMA

Yeah. You should really tell them, though, all three of them, so they don't find out from the book.

LEO

I don't think my three jock kids will be perusing the nonfiction section anytime / soon.

EMMA

But you should still tell them.

LEO

I know. I will.

EMMA

Thanks for, uh...it's been really nice to be here.

(a warm pause)

LEO

You wanna try to get some sleep?

EMMA

Soon.

> (he begins to exit. Emma
> reads from a document.)

Senators, in all dignity, in all self-respect, in all loyalty to the constitution and to this country, I could not participate in the purposes of this committee.

                              LEO

What's that?

                              EMMA

It's your dad.

> (she holds out the testimony
> to him)

His testimony before the subcommittee.
> (he doesn't come toward her)

                              LEO

Where did you get it?

                              EMMA

Federal repository on Madison Avenue. Any of us could have gotten it anytime. I just said Joe Joseph and they came back five minutes later with...but I couldn't bring myself to read it, the whole bus ride up here, I just...

> (he takes it hesitantly)

                              LEO

Oh, man.
"In all dignity, in all self-respect..."

                              EMMA

He says some really wonderful things. Really brave.

                              LEO

God, I can hear his, his –

EMMA

Yeah, I know.

LEO

You remember / his — ?

EMMA

A little. I remember being scared of him and thinking he
was the smartest person in the world.

>   (she sees that he is immersed
>   in the document.)

It's amazing, how they keep hounding him, they ask the
same question about two hundred/ different –

LEO
>   (reading, imitating his father)
Gentleman, that is the same question, and I have already
answered it.

EMMA

What was your answer?

LEO

I decline to answer!
>   (they laugh)
That's terrible, your dad does a great / Joe Joseph.

EMMA

No, it's good, it's good. I don't remember that well, he was
so sick by the time I was...
I should stop you there. In a few pages it gets really
disappointing.

LEO

Why?

EMMA

He perjures himself. He flat out denies committing
espionage, multiple times, they don't even ask the direct
question, he just volunteers...

(he flips forward a few pages,
finds it)

LEO

Hm.

EMMA

So.

LEO

Has Benny seen this?

EMMA

I don't know. It turns out there's a lot *Benny* never
shared with me.

(Leo looks at the front page
again)

LEO

May 19th, 1953.

EMMA

So you were...five? Dad was three. Janie would've
been...I guess your mom was pregnant?

LEO

Well that's true. But what I was thinking was. The
Rosenbergs were executed three weeks later.

(This had not occurred to
Emma. They are silent. He
hands the testimony back to
her.)

Make me a copy?

>   (she nods absent-mindedly.
>   He kisses the top of her head,
>   then starts to exit. He stops)

LEO

When I was in kindergarten we made kites. As a project,
arts and crafts. The teacher said we had to bring in, I
don't know, fifty cents each, to pay for our materials, the
kite sticks. I said, no need for that, I'll provide all the kite
sticks for everyone; you see, my dad owns a lumberyard.

EMMA

What?

LEO

We lived near a lumberyard, I don't know, I got confused,
or I was...building my dad up, bragging, you know, kid
stuff. So I went home and told him we needed to get all
those kite sticks. And his face. Just. Fell. He had been
out of work for years. All those kite sticks, we didn't have
any money.

EMMA

What did he do?

LEO

What could he do? He wasn't gonna hang me out to dry
like that. He bought the kite sticks. My mom must have
been furious. That must have been a fight. Shit, that
must have been a big fight. I keep thinking about that.
Anyway, sleep well.

>   (Leo exits. End scene.)

Scene ten.

Emma's apartment. Emma
and Miguel, late at night.

EMMA
And I *hated* my grandma Tessie, I didn't even go see her
when she was dying, because the myth I grew up with
was she left Joe at the height of the blacklist for some rich
guy, I mean that wasn't a myth, it was true, but I realize
now she must have *known* he spied, she must have
thought he brought this on himself, and her, and *three
young kids*, who *she* was supporting while he couldn't
work, and she didn't see it as noble, she saw it as stupid,
and irresponsible, and just think, as everything was
starting to come out about what was happening under
Stalin, and she must have thought – for this? We are
destitute? My *children* are destitute? She was seven
months pregnant and he was standing up there, *denying*
–

(the phone rings)

Don't answer that.

(they wait out. It stops.)

EMMA (VO)
You've reached Emma Jos –

(dial tone. Emma plunges on)

EMMA
And the legend about Vera, how she met him when he
was penniless and suicidally depressed because he had no
job, no marriage, he had lost hope in the beautiful dream
that was the revolution, and she accepted him; she was
proud to be with a man who stood before the committee
and took the fifth. But now that I've read the testimony I

know he didn't always take the fifth; he also lied. And I think it's very likely that Vera knew that too. So their marriage, it was like this tiny fortress against, against, against what had emerged to be a terrible mistake. Which they never acknowledged.

MIGUEL

May I say something?

EMMA

Yeah.

MIGUEL

Joe worked for the OSS during the war, that's when he was passing information.

EMMA

Uh-huh.

MIGUEL

What did he do there? I mean, what was he privy to that mattered to the Soviets?

EMMA

Well he was an economist in the Japanese division, and he also, apparently, befriended some people in the Soviet division so he was passing intelligence about both.

MIGUEL

And this was useful to the USSR how?

EMMA

I don't know *exactly* how, I haven't been able to get the specifics, but I can imagine that he would have gleaned from his colleagues in the Soviet division some – I don't know, strategies, or – that the US was keeping from the Soviet Union.

MIGUEL

But they were our allies.

EMMA

Yes, but you don't share everything you know, even with
your allies.

MIGUEL

I'm just not hearing anything that sounds that significant.

EMMA

Well obviously the Soviets felt it was significant because
they kept working with him.

MIGUEL

Was he paid?

EMMA

No! And that is not the point!

MIGUEL

I'm just trying to get all the information.

EMMA

He. Spied. He stood up and testified – okay, you know
the picture hanging over my desk in our office? That
picture, where he looks so broken, but so – I thought –
noble – on the day that picture was taken, he took an
oath, and then he –

> (she flips through the
> testimony)

he said, listen to this, he said, "Gentleman, may you know
this too, that I have never committed espionage!"

MIGUEL

So you're upset that he perjured himself.

EMMA

I'm – of course I'm upset that he perjured himself, but I'm
also upset that – and the point is not that *I'm* upset, it's a
matter of principle, that we honored him, we believed that

he upheld the constitution by fighting for what he
believed, openly, lawfully, and he was persecuted for *that*.
So if that basic premise is a lie then what is it exactly that
we are doing here?

MIGUEL

Emma, there is an innocent man on death row fifty years
after all this bullshit with your grandparents went / down
—

EMMA

Bullshit?

MIGUEL

Yes, and you have made yourself a key figure in the fight
to free this man, and you have not returned a single
phone call to *anyone* in two weeks, including a man who is
trying to leave us four million dollars. So I'm very
interested in the psychodrama of your family, but I'm also
wondering some things, like, do I still have a job?

EMMA

Four million / dollars?

MIGUEL

That's the figure Morty's accountant quoted me, yeah.

(pause. Emma takes this in)

I mean that's...that's a game changer.

EMMA

Holy shit, yeah.

MIGUEL

I'm not having a tough time thinking of things we could
do with four / million dollars.

EMMA

Oh my God, Miguel.

MIGUEL

Listen, stop me if I'm like way over the line here, Em, but
I think what's happening, with the book – it could
actually be really good for you. And for us.

(she stares at him)

I mean, I think it's about time you put some distance
between yourself and your family.

EMMA

Okay.

MIGUEL

It's just, it's a different time now and I think maybe this
will help you move forward in a really healthy way.
Making the connection between Mumia and the blacklist
was so smart, I mean it got the Morty's of the world
involved, and you having this personal story
obviously...but maybe at this point, it's, I don't know.
Time to let that go a little.

EMMA

I see.

(he registers that this is
really not going well and
back-pedals)

MIGUEL

Don't get me wrong, I have a ton of respect for your
grandfather and his whole / generation –

EMMA

Uh-huh.

MIGUEL

I mean I don't think we can even know what they were up
against, what those times were/ like.

EMMA

You've been an activist for about five minutes, Miguel, you actually really don't know anything.

(pause)

MIGUEL

Well that's not true. And I think making our work more about Mumia and less about 1953 is not the worst idea. But I just work here. So I guess I'll go to the office and wait until you make up your mind.

(he exits. Lights shift)

Scene eleven.

Ben on Emma's answering
machine

BEN

My question is are you not picking up your phone for
anyone or did you get caller ID just to avoid me? Or are
you screening? Are you listening to me, right now?
Pick up the phone, Emma. This is your dad and you're
hurting me a lot. Please pick up the phone.
                    (pause.)
I was reelected president of the teachers' union this week.
I know you think it's time I retired and let somebody
young with new ideas step in, maybe a woman or
somebody of color, but honey, nobody with any real vision
came forward and there was a lot of pressure on me to run
again so I caved and I did. This is the kind of thing I'd
usually like to talk to you about, see if you think I did the
right thing.
Emma? If you're there? Please?
                    (Emma seems like she might
                    pick up. Then, angrily)
Okay, since this fucking machine is the only way to talk to
you, let me tell you a few things you might not have
thought of. When he first got involved in the spying,
we're barely out of the depression, that meant *thirty
percent* unemployment, it meant you don't walk past a
garbage can without someone elbow deep in it. This is the
landscape of my father's childhood and young adulthood.
Now who are the people speaking up on behalf of the
destitute? The American Communist Party. Who is
talking about racial equality, twenty-five years before the
civil rights movement? Same answer. Who is calling
attention to the fact that Russians are dying by the
millions fighting fascism so that American hands can stay
clean? Same answer, Emma. So who is my dad's
allegiance to? Is it to J. Edgar Fucking Hoover? Is it to a
president who fully intends to sell out the Soviets once

Hitler is out of the way? No, it's to his party, it's to the honest working class Russians who are dying so that he can be free. So that his kids, and their kids, that's *you*, could be free. You want to condemn him from where you're sitting, kiddo, from your upper west side / apartment, fine, but he's my father and I want nothing to do with it.

                    MEL
                       (having come upon him)

Ben!
                       (gently)

Benji, Benji, Benji.

                       (she takes the phone from him
                       and hangs it up)

                    END ACT

PLAYWRIGHTS
HORIZONS

Ben and Emma • Peter Friedman and Katharine Powell

Ben, Leo, Mel, Emma, and Vera
Peter Friedman, Mark Blum, Mare Winningham, Katharine Powell, and Lois Smith

PLAYWRIGHTS HORIZONS

Emma and Morty • Katharine Powell and David Margulies

Ben and Mel • Peter Friedman and Mare Winningham

Emma and Miguel • Katharine Powell and Elliot Villar

All photos by Joan Marcus

ACT II

Scene one.

> Emma's apartment. Emma
> is in PJ's, smoking.
> Miguel enters, quietly. She
> doesn't hear him.

MIGUEL

Hey.

> (she turns)

EMMA

Hey.

MIGUEL

I've been trying to call you.

EMMA

You have?

MIGUEL

Yeah, I think your phone's off the hook.

EMMA

Oh.

MIGUEL

> (finding the phone indeed off
> the hook, and replacing it)

"Oh."

> (the phone immediately rings.
> Emma shakes her head. They
> wait it out. It stops ringing.)

EMMA

It's good to see you.

MIGUEL

Yeah, you too.

EMMA

I have been feeling so terrible about /what I said.

MIGUEL

I know.

EMMA

No, let me say this, because it was actually completely not representative – it's not how I feel. At all.

MIGUEL

I know that, Em.

EMMA

Because I have so much respect for your work, I'm sure I haven't said enough that I think you have a fucking incredible political mind, and the left is very lucky to have you.

MIGUEL

I've also been told I have an amazing face.

EMMA

Miguel, I'm being serious.

MIGUEL

I know you are.

EMMA

I'm trying to tell you that I admire you, *so much*, and you've taught me a lot.

MIGUEL
(truly)

Thank you.

EMMA

And I also think we've been really equal partners up to
this point.
(brief pause)

MIGUEL
(unconvincingly, but really
trying not to start a fight)

Yyyyeah.

EMMA

Oh.

MIGUEL

No, in a lot of ways, yeah.

EMMA

You don't feel that way.

MIGUEL

Well...I work for you. I mean, it's your fund and I work
for you.
I didn't think that was a controversial statement.

EMMA

It may not be, but it still makes me feel like shit, to hear
you say it like that.

MIGUEL

How would you say it?

EMMA

I say you work *with* me. When people ask, that's what I
say.

MIGUEL

But that's a euphemism. Isn't it?
(brief pause)
It hasn't bothered me, for the most part, I mean I'm a
modern guy, and it is your fund, I came in / late.

EMMA
It obviously bothers you.

MIGUEL
Now it bothers me, yeah, when I'm trying to get Mumia off death row and home to his son and you're sitting here in your pajamas pitying your –
Sorry. Sorry. I didn't come here to get into another fight.
> (he hands her a document)

We finished a draft of the petition. Leonard wants your notes.
I told him you have the flu. Nasty, stubborn, 1918 style flu. I told him you'd be back at work any day.
> (she stares at the document)

EMMA
Do you think he's innocent?

MIGUEL
Who?

EMMA
Mumia.

MIGUEL
...what?

EMMA
I've been wondering. I've been wondering about a lot of things.

MIGUEL
> (calmly)

I think he didn't receive a fair trial. I think he was railroaded by a racist judge, jury, and prosecution. I think there's no way he'd be on death row if here weren't an outspoken political black man.

EMMA

Granted, but isn't it pretty likely he killed Daniel
Faulkner? I just keep thinking, even though we're right
about so many things, we're right he was railroaded, we're
right the death penalty is racist, we're right the
government systematically punishes vocal progressives,
but even being right about all those things, the end result
could be that we free a man who's guilty of murder.

MIGUEL

He's not guilty.

EMMA

But if he is?

(The phone rings. Miguel
impulsively picks up)

MIGUEL

Hello?

EMMA

No-no-no!

(lights up on Ben)

BEN

Hello! Hi. Miguel. Oh good, hi. It's Ben, Emma's dad.

MIGUEL

Hi Ben.

(Emma shaking her head)

BEN

Como estás?

MIGUEL

Good. Uh, good. How are you?

BEN

I've been better. As I'm sure you know. Is Emma there?

>   (Miguel looks pleadingly to
>   Emma, who turns away)

MIGUEL

She is here. I'm, uh. I'm not sure if she's gonna get on
the phone. Sorry.

BEN

Not your fault.
>   (pause)
You guys getting to relax at all? Going to the beach, or...

MIGUEL

No. Well, yeah, a couple weeks ago we went to this thing,
it's called Midsummer Night Swing.

BEN

Midsummer Night Swing?

MIGUEL

At Lincoln Center, it's uh. Swing dancing, you know, they
hire a / band...

BEN

Emma does swing dancing?

MIGUEL

No, no she really doesn't. At all. I don't either, but I can
fake it. She...it was pretty funny.
>   (Miguel is looking at Emma.
>   She looks back at him.)

BEN

Yeah?

MIGUEL

Yeah.

BEN

Well I'm glad she has you.
(pause)
Has she made any decisions about the fund? If it's okay
to ask.

MIGUEL

No. She hasn't.

BEN

She, uh. When we first spoke about it there was some
talk about renaming it; I'm hoping that was just, you
know, heat of the moment stuff.
(brief pause)

MIGUEL

No, I don't think so.

BEN

Because, the idea that all these years later, she has to
apologize for her grandfather's radical politics – that's, I
don't know at your age if you can understand this, that's
just the scariest kind of history repeating itself.

MIGUEL

But she wouldn't be apologizing for Joe's radical politics.
She'd be apologizing that he spied for Stalin.
(Emma's hand flies to her
mouth. Ben reeling.)

BEN

Well thanks for pickin' up.

MIGUEL

I wish there was something I could do.
(Brief pause)

BEN

Tell her, uh. Tell her I'm sorry about that last message.
And I'm not gonna call again. Since I guess that's what
she wants.

(Ben hangs up. Miguel
hangs up)

MIGUEL

He —

EMMA

Please don't tell me. I don't want to know.
(Leo enters Ben's space —
Ben's head in his hands.)

LEO

Hey.
(Ben looks up)
Sammy has that baseball game today, I wasn't sure if you
still wanted to come. I was gonna call, but I thought my
chances would be better if I just showed up.

BEN

Is he pitching?

LEO

He's gonna try. He's having trouble with that shoulder.

BEN

Oh no, still?

LEO

Yeah, Beth's having a fit, but last game of the year, I
couldn't say no.
He loves it when you come, you know. The way you make
a fool of yourself yelling his name in the stands. That's
one thing I've never been any good at, cheering at sports
games.

BEN
(not a mean-spirited joke)
Luckily that's the only thing.
(Leo throws something at
him, if possible.)

LEO
Come on, it's a beautiful June day. What else you gonna
do, sit here and stew?

BEN
Yeah, I had at least two hours more stewing on the
agenda, followed by some brooding, and maybe a little
moping if there's time.

LEO
I'll get you home by seven; you can do all those things
then. It would mean a lot to him.
(the answer seems to be yes. Then —)

BEN
Emma stayed with you, while she was in Boston.

LEO
I'm sorry, she asked me not to tell you.
(Ben nods)
Should I have said no? What would you have done?

BEN
I would've called you. Your kid? I would've called you.

LEO
I didn't know what good it would do; she's / an adult.

BEN
Still, I would have liked to know.

LEO
I can understand that.
(brief pause)

I told my own kids about the book, I sat the three of them
down together, I might as well have said, you know, corn
prices are falling in Kentucky. They were just...
No reaction. And I realized that's what I had been afraid
of – not that they would be upset, but that they wouldn't.
Because that's my fault, I guess I didn't instill, or. I failed
to get something across about who dad was, about who I
am. Beth thought it was "interesting," that's it. She
meant from a psychological standpoint. She always said
dad was needy, that he required a lot of praise, so it made
sense to her, she said, that he would have done that. God
I got so fucking defensive, I don't know why, her calling
him needy, wiping out the whole historical – everything,
with a little pop psychology, I just...
So anyway, Emma's been sort of the only person I can
really talk to about it.

                    BEN
Lucky you.

                    LEO
I'm not saying that as a barb, just so you / understand.

                    BEN
You may not intend it as a barb but it feels like a barb.

                    LEO
I'd like to be able to talk to *you* about it, that's the point.

                    BEN
I don't see us ever agreeing.

                    LEO
There's a lot we agree about, you're focused on a very
minor / part of the story.

                    BEN
We're talking about the difference between honoring dad
and shitting on him, that's what we're talking about.

LEO

I guess that's the main thing we disagree about; that
those are the only two options.
(pause)

BEN

I appreciate your coming by. But I don't think I'm gonna
come to the game.

LEO
(sadly)

Okay.

BEN

Tell him good luck. Uh, tell him watch that shoulder.
(Leo exits. Mel enters)

MEL

Was that Leo?

BEN

He wanted me to go to Sammy's game.

MEL

Oh Benji, you should've gone.

BEN

Well. Add that to the list.

MEL

Please don't snap at me. I don't deserve that.

BEN

I'm getting a little tired of hearing from you about the
things I should've done.

MEL

You asked me! You asked me what I thought, and I told
you. Am I not allowed to have an opinion? I think you

should've told her earlier, I do. But you didn't, so we're in
this, and we deal with it, and notice I say we.
(pause)

BEN

Miguel picked up. Just now.
He said...he said he took Emma swing dancing. Can you
picture that?

(Mel can't.)

MIGUEL

I think we should take a break.

EMMA

What?
What do you mean?
(pause)
Well I don't think so. I don't think we should.

MIGUEL

Uh...

EMMA

I think you're overreacting. I mean can we talk about
this?

MIGUEL

We can talk about it, but I know that's what I want.

EMMA

Well I completely disagree.

MIGUEL

I'm sorry to hear that, but in this kind of situation, the
person who wants to take a break wins. That's just how it
works.

EMMA

What do you mean by 'a break?'

MIGUEL

You could make this a little easier for me, Em.

EMMA

Are you breaking up with me?

MIGUEL

I don't know.

EMMA

What do you mean you don't know?

MIGUEL

You're letting me down, okay? You're not acting like I ever thought you would act. And I need to think about whether I want us to make it through this.
(pause)

EMMA

Well if it makes a difference I do want us to make it through this. I don't need to think about that because I know.

MIGUEL

It does make a difference. But I still need to think.
(He picks up the petition)

MIGUEL

Will you read this?

EMMA

Honestly? Probably not.

(Sadly, he takes the petition with him. He exits.)

Scene two.

>   Emma and Morty at Gene's
>   restaurant. They have
>   finished eating and the check
>   is on the table.

>   A long pause. Morty's face a
>   mask of pained kindness.

MORTY

Well.

>   (pause.)

EMMA

This morning I received my first nasty email about it from
a, um, right wing... someone with an advance copy. But it
comes out on Friday, so. More people are going to notice.

MORTY

Yes. They will.

>   (pause)

EMMA

I hardly think I need to say that you're released from any
pledge you may have made to the fund.

MORTY

Oh, / Emma.

EMMA

The last time we sat here you asked me not to make a
fuss. I'm asking you not to, now. Let's just forget that
whole thing.

MORTY

Emma.

EMMA

And please apologize to your accountant for me; I'm sorry
I wasted his time.

MORTY

Listen —

EMMA

That's all. That's all. Okay?

            (Emma takes the check from
            the edge of the table and
            opens it)

MORTY

What are you doing?

EMMA

I'm buying you lunch.

MORTY

I won't hear of that.

EMMA

It's the least I can do.

MORTY

Give that to me.

            (Emma puts her credit card
            in the check)

EMMA

It's done.

MORTY

Emma Joseph, you take that card back and you give that
to me.
            (cowed, she does)

I don't understand this attitude. I don't understand it at all.

Am I to believe that this...detail about your grandfather's biography. Leaves you totally uninterested in continuing your work?

EMMA

It's not a question of being interested, Morty, I just can't continue.

MORTY

So you're putting an end to the fund. Is that what you're telling me?

EMMA

I don't see another choice.

MORTY

I am simply amazed.

EMMA

And I'm surprised, too, to hear you refer to what I just told you as a "detail." Considering the – well, the faith you put in my grandfather's legacy. I would think this would be pretty devastating to you, too, actually.

MORTY

And when did you hear me say that your grandfather never spied for the Soviets? When did I say that?
(brief pause)

EMMA

You — ?

MORTY

No, I didn't know.
But sure, I knew.
We're talking the 1940's? Take a walk in the East Village, throw a stone you hit a spy. I mean you didn't *say* that. You say that you sound a lot like a certain

Senator from Wisconsin who you do not want to sound like. But...

> (a gesture to say "it was true")

Mostly we're talking about nothing, we're talking about, I don't know, a good recipe for soap. You have a good recipe for soap, you mention it to somebody else in the party, next thing you know you're meeting a guy named Nikolai on a bench, handing over your soap recipe so some Russian kids can have a nice bath. This is the kind of thing that would later be called "spying" and for these people life would become hell. Now your grandfather was in government, so that's different. It did not help the left in the long run what he and his colleagues, what they did.

EMMA

No.

MORTY

No. So, that's a lesson. And we move on. Right?

> (brief pause)

EMMA

The story I was raised with was that it was the government that lied, and cheated, and conspired.

MORTY

Still true.

EMMA

Still true, yes, but Joe met Soviet Agents under highway overpasses and handed over unmarked envelopes; he had a *code name*; that was not what I heard on my father's knee.

MORTY

You're disappointed, I understand. You're disappointed in your family. It's terrible, I know, but Emma, this is not an uncommon predicament.

And you ask me, it's not a reason to let down Mumia, to let down all the people you have promised to help.
But I see your heart is no longer in it, and I will speak to my accountant and my lawyer later today, if that's what you want.

(brief pause)

EMMA

I'm trying really hard to figure out what the right thing to do is, Morty.

MORTY

It can be hard, can't it? Even for very bright, well-meaning people. In a tough situation, to know what's right?

Scene three.

Emma late at night. Her
phone rings. It could be
Miguel. She answers.

EMMA

Hello?

MEL

Hi honey.
         (brief pause)

EMMA

Mel?

MEL

Don't hang up, okay?
         (brief pause)
Your dad's asleep, it's just me calling.
How are you?

EMMA

Fine.

MEL

Good. I'm fine too. Your sister is doing really well, I don't
know if you've talked to her recently, she's...I know better
than to feel sure of anything, but it's just incredible, how
far she's come.
The dogs are fine.

EMMA

Good.

MEL

I just, I'm calling because I want to tell you about the time
I did some civil disobedience, the *one* time, I don't think
I've ever told you about it because it's a pretty painful
memory / actually.

EMMA

Mel –

MEL

Honey just let me tell this story, okay?
It was the eighties, and it was for – never mind what it
was for, who remembers, and I got put in jail, for, I don't
know, a day, two days. You have to keep in mind, Emma,
I'm a nice girl from the Midwest, this is *way* – being in
jail, I'm terrified, I'm uncomfortable, I'm having panic
attacks. Long story short your dad picks me up directly
from jail once I'm released, we've been together maybe a
year but it's before I moved in with you guys. And he
takes me to Joe and Vera's. And I'm thinking, this is
gonna be *great*, because whereas my own republican
parents don't understand what the fuck I'm doing with my
life, Ben's parents get it. And they'll be *proud*. And this
is my new *family*. You know?

EMMA

Uh-huh.

MEL

So we get there. We get there, and Emma, they never
fucking mentioned it.
They went on and on about Leo, and especially Ben, and
their political involvement and how they were so proud of
their sons. And they didn't say one word to me about
what I had done. What I had just been through.

EMMA

Why not?

MEL

Well when we left, I said, Benji, I was so hurt, I said,
"why didn't they say anything?" And he said, "the
communist party didn't approve of the cause you went to
jail for."

(pause)

You know it hurt your dad too, the way they treated me, and I didn't blame him at the time. But looking back, I think why didn't *he* say anything? Why didn't he stand up to his dad and say he was proud of me?
Kiddo, I want to say to you that I'm proud of you. I know what you're doing right now is hard and I'm proud of you.

                    EMMA
                  (in tears)
Thank you.

                    MEL
But I also have to say that what you're putting your dad through is cruel. Yell at him, curse, whatever, but you have to talk to him.

                    EMMA
I can't.

                    MEL
It's gonna be fuckin' hard. But yes you can.

                         (pause. Big deliberate mood
                         shift.)

Okay, end of speech, how's Miguel?

                    EMMA
Fine. No, not really fine, he's possibly very likely breaking up with me.

                    MEL
Why?

                    EMMA
I have no idea. I guess because I'm neglectful and self-righteous and can't admit when I'm wrong.

                         (Mel laughs)

MEL

Well, you're a Joseph. You have some good qualities too.

(brief pause)

EMMA

Thanks for calling, Mel.

MEL

Love to you, kiddo. From both of us, *love to you*.

(End scene)

> Scene four. Jess and Emma
> in front of Ben and Mel's
> house. Emma stops short.

JESS

You need a minute?

EMMA

Yeah. You can go in.

JESS

It's cool, I'll wait with you.
> (Jess takes out a cigarette.
> She offers one to Emma)

EMMA

No thanks.

> (Jess puts the pack away.
> Emma goes into Jess's bag,
> takes out the pack, and takes
> a cigarette. Jess gives her
> the gift of not remarking on
> this. She lights Emma's
> cigarette)

JESS

Remember when I broke my leg sneaking out of that window?

EMMA

Do I remember? Oh my god, I felt so terrible.

JESS

That sucked.

EMMA

And you told dad that I was asleep and didn't know you were sneaking out, and I never told him the truth, I still

feel awful when I think about that. You were in that
horrible contraption for what seemed like years.

                    JESS
Three breaks in one leg.

                    EMMA
Oh no.

                         (a wave of nausea)

                    JESS
Are you okay?

                    EMMA
...yeah. Thought I was gonna throw up for a second
there.

                    JESS
You're that nervous?

                    EMMA
Shut up. No.
                         (pause)

                    JESS
You know, this whole ...thing. Has been really
interesting for me. Because I'm suddenly like the good
kid. I call every couple days, I come over for dinner, I'm
like the silver lining child for the first time in my life.

                    EMMA
You seem...really good.

                    JESS
                         (quietly pleased)
I'm um. Dating someone. Actually.

                    EMMA
That's great! For how long?

JESS

Well only about a week and a half, but it seems, um.
Yeah.

EMMA

I want to hear all about him.

JESS

Uh-huh. Right. Um, *her.*

EMMA

... *what?*

JESS

Yeah. Yeah.

EMMA

Shit, you really are the silver lining child. Is dad thrilled
beyond belief?

JESS
(laughing with real joy and
hilarity)

Yes! Completely!

EMMA
(a little sadly)

Wow.

JESS

Come on, it wouldn't kill you to be happy for me.

EMMA

I am happy for you. What's her name?

JESS

Leaf. She's a batik artist, and she's the most
compassionate person I've ever known.

EMMA

That's, uh...
You deserve this.

JESS

Right??

(pause)
You ready? It won't be so bad; I'll be right there with you.

EMMA

It's funny; "Question Authority" was like a mantra we
were raised with, but somehow that never extended to
questioning *him*. For me, anyway.

JESS

For you.

(Jess stands. She pulls
Emma to her feet)

Scene five
Ben and Mel's house in
Brookline. Ben, Mel, Jess,
and Emma standing around
awkwardly. A silence in
which multiple people try to
think of what to say.

MEL

...and the bus?

EMMA

Was fine. Jess was actually on time to pick me up, so that
blew my mind.

JESS

I was *early*.

(they laugh)

MEL

Are you hungry?

EMMA

No.

BEN

Jess?

JESS

Not yet.

(another silence)

MEL

So I'm just gonna come out and ask, do you two want to be
alone? Or should we stay?

BEN

It's up to Emma.

EMMA

It doesn't matter.

JESS

It's up to you guys.

(Ben and Emma look at each other; no decision)

MEL

Well can I say what I think? I think you should be alone.

JESS

I told Emma I'd be with her if she wants.

MEL

That's fine too. Is that what you want, Emma?

EMMA

This is really weird and formal.

(brief pause)

MEL

Okay, I'm going to say again, though it's really not up to me, that my suggestion would be that you have this conversation alone.

BEN

That's okay with me.

JESS

Emma?

EMMA

Sure, whatever.

BEN

Not whatever, you should say what you want.

EMMA

Alone is fine. That's what I want.

MEL

Okay.

JESS
(quietly, just to Emma)

You sure?

(Emma nods)

MEL
(stagily)

Excuse me, everyone, I need to do something upstairs.
Jess, would you mind helping me do something upstairs?
(they make their way toward
the exit)
We are just upstairs. Should you need us.

(they exit. Silence.)

EMMA

You moved the picture of Fidel.

BEN

I figured no one got to see it in the bedroom, where it was.

(pause. They speak
simultaneously)

EMMA

/ So we should –

BEN

How are you?

EMMA

What?

BEN

How are you? Just. How have you been?

EMMA

I'm okay. How are you?

BEN

Well...

> (an attempt to smile through
> his misery is an answer to the
> question. A pause. Emma
> takes out a piece of paper.)

EMMA

I want to make sure I don't forget anything.

> (Ben nods, perhaps sits,
> readies himself to listen.
> Emma refers to her list.)

I guess I didn't put these in a very sensible order.

BEN

That's okay. Whatever order you want is okay. I'm glad we're doing this.

EMMA

Um. The first thing I have written down is that I don't like the way you talk about the guys I date. I don't like it when you speak Spanish in relation to them, I don't like when you brag to your friends that I only date Latino men. I don't understand why that should be a point of pride to you.

BEN

Sweetheart, no matter *who* you date it's a point of pride to me, everything you do is a point of pride to me.

EMMA

I recognize the truth of that, on one hand, and you should recognize the truth of what I said.

BEN

I just –

EMMA

Dad, that's just the first one.
                    (he accepts this and listens)
The second one. I'm skipping that one for now.
Oh. Number three is really small. It's that when I was
little you made me call my walkman a "walkperson." I
don't know why I...[included that]
Um. Number four
                    (shakily)
Is that you didn't tell me grandpa Joe was a spy.
Number five is that you raised me to believe the
revolution was coming and everything would be different
even though you knew that was not true.
Number six is that it took you so long to realize Jess
needed help. Because individual suffering has no place in
Marxist philosophy.
Number seven is that you always rewarded me for my
politics, and for working so hard, but never for just taking
a break. And thinking. And being doubtful. And being
sad.
Number eight is that I'm sorry.
Number nine. Um. I wrote again that you didn't tell me
grandpa Joe was a spy, I guess I forgot I had written that
already.
And number ten
                    (trouble reading it through
                    tears?)
Oh. Is that after Mel was in jail for civil disobedience in
the eighties you didn't tell Joe you were proud of her.

                    (she puts down the piece of
                    paper.)

BEN
          (a deeply painful but real
          attempt to joke)

After the Revolution   121

That's *it?*

EMMA

I don't expect you to respond to all of it right away.

BEN

I'm going to respond. I'm going to respond to numbers
four and nine first, since they were the same.
Uh.
I should've told you. I should've told you.
I have no excuse. I would like to explain the reasons,
which are different from excuses, for why I didn't tell you,
but only if you want to hear them.

EMMA

I don't know, Dad.

BEN

Up to you. No strings.

EMMA

Okay, what are the reasons?

> (Ben takes out a piece of
> paper. The slightest
> acknowledgement between
> the two of them that this is
> funny)

BEN

My dad didn't talk about it to us. He didn't even make an
allusion to it until I was, I don't know, about your age.
You can say that's because he felt he had done something
wrong, that there was some shame there, and that may be
true. But what's also true is that he was a man who lived
in terror. Our phones were tapped, FBI agents hung out
not far from our front door. The silence, that wasn't just a
parental choice. That was a strategy for keeping him out
of jail. And long after it was necessary, it was something
that was trained into him. And I guess I picked that up.

EMMA

You told Jess. You told her almost four years ago.

BEN

That's true, and as I said these are not excuses. Not for nothing I didn't tell her on American soil.

EMMA

On — ? Dad!

BEN

You can call it paranoid.

EMMA

I do, I do call it paranoid.

BEN

But that was part of my thinking. The second reason is that around the time I was planning to tell you, you started the Joe Joseph fund. You called and asked me to be on your board, you remember that? You said I was your "first ask." When you have kids maybe you'll know what that feels like, I *hope* you'll know what the feels like, to have a child grow up and say I've thought about it, and I believe what you believe, and I want you to be a part of it.

EMMA

You should have told me during that conversation.

BEN

But you had this powerful analysis about Mumia, and McCarthy, and the way this country still punishes the outspoken, that was so *smart*, I didn't want to. I don't know. Muddy the waters. Because what you were saying was right, the details of the history notwithstanding, it was still right, and people were paying attention.

EMMA

You're saying it was true despite the fact that it was partly a lie.

BEN

No, I'm saying –

EMMA

Dad, that's what you're saying. I need you to see that.

(pause)

BEN

And the last reason was, uh. A tremendous fear of letting you down. Which I have felt since you were three and a half, right after your mom left us, and I was a complete wreck. And you asked me very frankly one morning if I was too sad to take care of you and Jess.

EMMA

I don't remember that.

BEN

Good.
I heard your list. I heard it, and I'm trying to learn. Even at my age.
But I never made you call it a walkperson; that / is fucking crap.

EMMA

You — ?!! You did!

BEN

I did not.

EMMA

If I wanted one for the ecumenical winter holiday I had to call it a walkperson, you must remember that.

                              BEN

Nope.

                             EMMA

Well.
You did.

                           (pause)

                              BEN

What was two? If I dare ask.

                             EMMA

Hm?

                              BEN

You skipped number two.

                             EMMA

Oh.
                           (she looks at the paper,
                           though she doesn't have to)
it wasn't important.

                              BEN

While we're getting it all out there we should be thorough.

                             EMMA

It's just...uh.
That I sometimes smoke. That's all.
And I'm twenty-six and I don't want to be sneaking
around hiding it from you. So.

                           (a long pause. Ben has to
                           squelch about a hundred
                           impulses to lecture, berate,
                           plead, etc. He settles on)

                              BEN

Thanks for telling me.

Have you decided what you're going to do with the fund?

                         EMMA
I have.

                         BEN
Okay.
                         (he realizes she's not going to
                         tell him)
Okay.

Scene Six
Vera's apartment. Emma
reads to Vera.

EMMA

Dear Friends of The Joe Joseph Fund. Uh... I'm gonna
skip the introduction. Okay. You okay?

VERA

So far you haven't said anything.

EMMA

The first order of business is that it has come to light that
my grandfather, Joe Joseph, passed classified government
information to Soviet Agents during World War II. This
fact came as a shock to –
(to Vera)
you know this part...
(continuing to read)
I realize your support for the fund may have been
intimately connected to Joe's legacy, and because of that
I'd like to offer you the chance to have your donations
returned. An anonymous donor has offered to make up
for any lost funds, so your decision to have your
contributions returned will not negatively impact our
work.
That said, I urge you not only to let your past
contributions stand, but to continue to make the Joe
Joseph Fund a financial priority. We have reached a
crucial juncture in the fight to free Mumia Abu-Jamal.
This fall we expect the Supreme Court to hear our
petition for –
(to Vera)
And I go on about Mumia for a while...um.....
(reading)
It turns out that my grandfather's legacy / included –

VERA

Louder.

EMMA
(loudly)
It turns out that my grandfather's legacy included
activities that I consider to be dishonest and dishonorable.
But it is his greater legacy, his belief in a society where
regardless of your race or political persuasion you may
speak out without fear, that I hope you will continue to
uphold with your contributions and your support.

The other piece of news is that I am resigning as
Executive Director of the fund. You can direct any
questions to Miguel Roja, our interim leader, whose
wisdom and passion will guide us through this period of
transition. I will retain my position on the board, and I
will never be far from this organization in my heart and
mind.

That's it.

(pause)

VERA
Well I think I know who the anonymous donor is. And I
hope he's not expecting a date out of this.

(Emma laughs)

I don't agree with a lot of it, but you know that.
I don't agree with your decision to leave it in someone
else's hands. It's a family thing, or that's what I thought.
And I don't know what you're going to do with yourself,
besides.

EMMA
I don't know either, Grandma.

VERA

And I don't agree with what you said about, uh.
Dishonorable. I don't agree with that at all, and I wish
you'd change it before you send it out.

EMMA

I've already sent it out.

VERA

Oh. Then you're not asking for my advice.

EMMA

No.

VERA

Then I'm not sure why you read it to me.

EMMA

I wanted to share it with you. The conclusions I've
reached.

VERA

Well. The fact is you weren't there back then so you can't
ever really know what it was like.   You can look back and
say we did this wrong, or we did that wrong, but the point
is it was *for* something. I look at most people your age, at
your cousins, and I don't know what they're for. I don't
know how they're going to feel when they get to be my
age. When they look back and see how they spent their
time. I look back and I feel proud.

EMMA

I feel proud too. Of you and Joe, and my dad, I feel very
proud.

VERA

Then why don't you say that in the letter?

EMMA

Grandma, I think I do. It makes me sad that you couldn't
hear that in it.

VERA

Well. Every relationship has some sadness in it, right?
That's life.

> (brief pause. She continues,
> not unkindly, but with
> incredible lucidity, as the
> lights fade imperceptibly.
> Emma listens.)

Listen, what you've done here, my darling, is you've
named your grandfather's name.
That's what it amounts to.
And – don't argue – you have your reasons, I understand
that, I understand how from your point of view it's about
honesty. But I met him after they named his name the
first time, and it was a horror, an absolute horror. He
spent the rest of his life recovering from that, but he
raised his children to be proud. And not to be afraid. And
to keep fighting. I spoke to your father, he told me he's
forgiven you. He said it's healthy for you to be critical of
your grandfather...he called that "progress." That's what
he said. Well. I've lived too long to call it progress,
Emma. And I love you and I'm sorry I can't agree with
you.
But progress?
I'm afraid not.
No.

(Black)